T0106159

THE
MONDAY
MORNING
CHURCH

Bus Stop

THE
MONDAY
MORNING
CHURCH

Out of the
SANCTUARY
and Into the
STREETS

 HOWARD
PUBLISHING CO

JERRY COOK

Author of *LOVE, ACCEPTANCE, AND FORGIVENESS*
Over 300,000 copies in print

OUR PURPOSE AT HOWARD PUBLISHING IS TO:
- *Increase* faith in the hearts of growing Christians
- *Inspire* holiness in the lives of believers
- *Instill* hope in the hearts of struggling people everywhere
  BECAUSE HE'S COMING AGAIN!

The Monday Morning Church © 2006 by Jerry Cook
All rights reserved. Printed in the United States of America
Published by Howard Publishing Co., Inc.
3117 North Seventh Street, West Monroe, Louisiana 71291-2227
www.howardpublishing.com

06 07 08 09 10 11 12 13 14 15   10 9 8 7 6 5 4 3 2 1

Edited by Michele Buckingham
Interior design by John Mark Luke Designs
Cover design by Matt Smart

Library of Congress Cataloging-in-Publication Data
Cook, Jerry O.
     The Monday morning church : out of the sanctuary and into the streets /
Jerry Cook.
        p. cm
     Includes bibliographical references (p.).
     ISBN 978-1-4516-3618-5
     1. Evangelistic work. 2. Christian life—Foursquare Gospel authors. 3.
Evangelistic work—Biblical teaching. 4. Christian life—Biblical teaching. 5.
Bible. N. T. Ephesians—Criticism, interpretation, etc. I. Title.

BV3790.C598 2006
269'.2—dc22
                                                                    2005055111

No part of this publication may be reproduced in any form without the prior
written permission of the publisher except in the case of brief quotations within
critical articles and reviews.

Scripture quotations not otherwise marked are from the *Holy Bible, New International Version* NIV®. Copyright © 1973, 1978, 1984 by International Bible Society. Used by permission of Zondervan Publishing House. All rights reserved. Scripture quotations marked NKJV are from *The Holy Bible, New King James Version*. Copyright © 1982, by Thomas Nelson, Inc. Used by permission. All rights reserved. Italics in Scripture quotations indicate author's added emphasis.

To Christi:
*the remarkable woman every father
prays his daughter will become.*

To Barbara:
my bride, my friend, and my life companion.

This book is the result of their love and dedication.

Table of
CONTENTS

Part 1: WHERE IS GOD ON MONDAY?

Part 2: WHO YOU ARE

Part 3: WHAT YOU HAVE

Part 4: HOW YOU LIVE

To Denny and Philis Boultinghouse of Howard Publishing; Denny for your enthusiasm and vision for the message of this book, Philis for keeping me on track and your continuing encouragement.

To Michele Buckingham for her remarkable skill and sensitivity in editing the material.

You all are professional, loving, and truly Christian.

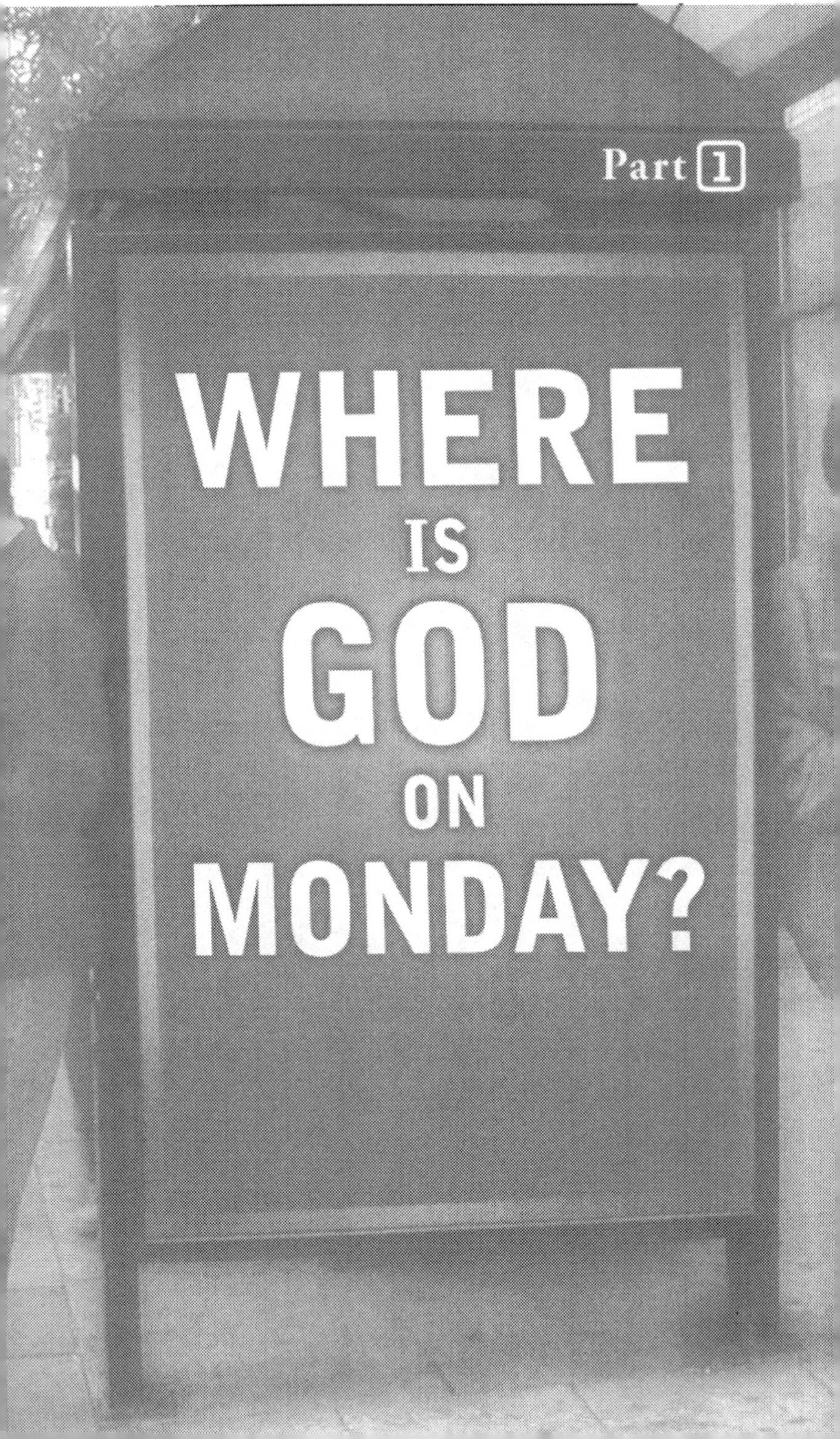

Part 1

WHERE IS GOD ON MONDAY?

The POWER of the CHURCH on Monday

The church on Sunday is great. I love it and enjoy it. But what I get really excited about is the church on Monday—the body of Christ at work in the world.

Some time ago I was given the book *The Christ of the Indian Road*, written in 1925 by Earl Stanley Jones, a Methodist missionary to India. Jones had been remarkably inept at making Methodists out of the people of India. Finally he decided to abandon his conventional Westernized missionary venture and, instead, "place Jesus on the Indian road" in a simple, clear, and unacculturated way. Furthermore, he determined not to demand a certain response to his message but to let each person decide what he or she would do about Jesus. The results were astounding, greatly influencing missionary strategies of the future.

"Christ is becoming a familiar Figure upon the Indian Road," Jones wrote. "He is becoming naturalized there. Upon the road of India's thinking you meet with him again and again, on the highways of India's affection you feel his gracious Presence, on the ways of her decisions and actions he is becoming regal and authoritative. And the voice of India is beginning to say with Whittier:

> The healing of His seamless dress
> Is by our beds of pain;
> We touch Him in life's throng and press,
> And we are whole again.[1]

It is this "placing of Christ on the road," whether in India or America, that is our crucial mission as Christians. We are called to make Jesus accessible to people, right where they live. It is also our only hope for effective evangelism that penetrates deep into the fiber of society. This mission requires an acceptance of certain basic principles:

- The essential gospel centers on the person of Christ, not the church, not even evangelism. The gospel is Jesus. He is the "good news." Everything else is vehicular to an accurate presentation of him.

- The church is "his body"—the body of Christ—"the fullness of him" (Ephesians 1:23). Of course, that's not the only statement in the New Testament about the nature of the church, but it is definitive when it comes to the church's presence in the world.

- The model for the church is Jesus. The Gospels give us a picture of the ministry of the church. What we see in the life of Christ is what we ought to be seeing in the life of the church.

- The book of Acts gives us an example of what happens when Christ is accurately placed in both the religious culture—

"in Jerusalem, and in all Judea and Samaria"—and secular cultures—"to the ends of the earth" (Acts 1:8). When and where the church has failed to carry on this approach, cultures have failed to be truly Christian. Tragically, the great majority of cultures we read about in the book of Acts are now Muslim. Part of the blame has to be laid at the doorstep of the institution the church has become.

- Christ's own incarnation teaches us that "incarnational Christianity" (the presence of Christ in culture) can only be accomplished by persons, not institutions. This is not to devalue institutions or organizations. It is to say, however, that the person of Jesus can only be clearly communicated through the people in whom he dwells.

- Colossians 1:19 tells us that the fullness of God is Jesus. Christ is the perfect model of what the word *incarnation* means. He is how God dwells in men. After this same model, we as Spirit-filled believers can now step into the incarnational experience. Jesus, of course, is the "only begotten of the Father" (John 1:14 NKJV), so we are not sons of God in the same way he is. However, we can look at Jesus to understand how the Holy Spirit joins himself to our humanity in a way that puts the treasure in clay pots (see 2 Corinthians 4:7) without devaluing the treasure or destroying the pots. He is present in us *at all times and in all locations.*

With these truths in mind, then, any effort to present Jesus as Savior must focus on the *church on Monday* rather than the *church on Sunday.* No matter how big the church on Sunday becomes, it will never penetrate the culture with Jesus. The reason is clear. The church on Sunday is experienced by the church community; it is only *observed* (if noticed at all) by the unbelieving community.

The church on Monday is an entirely different matter. It operates *in the experience* of nonbelievers. It lives on their turf, moves in their society, and operates in their culture. On Monday Jesus is "on the road." He ceases to be one of the characters in the program of the institution called church. Rather, he works beside people. He eats in their restaurants and banks at their branches. He has coffee in their front rooms and hangs out by their water coolers. He is in their lives. He is *incarnate*. And because he can be seen and touched, he can be received or rejected. True evangelism is possible.

Strategic Placement

Most Christians have been trained quite well to be the church on Sunday. But what does it take to train believers to be the church on Monday?

The first step is to help them recognize their strategic placement. By "strategic placement" I mean this: each redeemed, Spirit-filled Christian has been strategically placed by Jesus Christ, the Lord of the church. Where each believing man or woman lives and works is part of that strategy. Christians are people of destiny, purposely placed by God deep inside our culture. They are his points of incarnational penetration. Because of them Jesus is present at the very heart of society. And it is this strategic presence of Christ that opens the door for his revelation as Savior to an unbelieving world.

Incarnational Christianity doesn't try to get people to God.

Large numbers of men and women don't want to get to God. Others are unaware there is a God to get to! The incarnation was God coming to us; in a similar way, incarnational Christianity brings Jesus to men.

That's the basis for true evangelism: in the believer the presence of Christ reaches out to the unbeliever. It's also the basis for true discipleship: in the believer the presence of Christ walks alongside the new believer. Thus, the two main activities of the church—conversion and discipling—are wed, as they were meant to be. The Great Commission, after all, does not simply say to go into all the world and make converts; we are to go and make disciples.

Jesus said simply, "I am the way. If you have found me, you have found God." Unfortunately, somewhere along the line, the church added a debilitating step to the divine program. We said, "Jesus is the way to God, and the church is the way to Jesus. Come to the church and find Jesus, then Jesus will take you to God." Any training that we do, any leadership that we exert, must correct this error. We must never allow the church institution to be the way to Jesus. Jesus himself is the Way. The goal of the church on Monday is to make the Way present and visible in a world where people are lost. And, through incarnational Christianity, he is!

Open for Business

Of course, it does no good to have a strategic force in place if the people don't know they are strategic, don't know they are a force, and don't know they are in place. Most Christians, I think, give some kind of mental assent to this idea of strategic placement, but they have no concept of its implications or of their direct involvement. Some think in terms of inviting hurting people to a church program; others think of using some type of soul-winning gimmick to make a convert. Most, however, don't do anything with the idea at all. It simply floats around, untapped, in the background of their Christian experience. They're strategically placed, but they're not "open for business."

I'm convinced that if more Christians would get open for business, then more business would begin showing up. The question is, how can believers get informed, affirmed, equipped, and open for business, so that the business of Christ in the world can take place through them?

This question brings up several important issues to consider, both for individual believers and for the church community. If incarnational Christianity is going to have an impact, individual believers must:

1. Redefine ministry (both as to content and location)

2. Redefine church (both as to function and identity)

3. Reevaluate their reasons for being a part of the church community

4. Rethink their reasons for work

5. Reestablish the distinction between profession (the way they earn a living) and vocation (their destiny—being Jesus in their world)

The church community must:

1. Redefine leadership

2. Redefine success

3. Redefine purpose

4. Begin with the church on Monday and work toward Sunday

5. Ask, "What does the church on Monday need to accomplish its ministry?"

6. Ask, "What does the church on Monday need when it gathers on Sunday?"

Confidence, Courage, and Trust

Many years ago I wrote a book with Stanley Baldwin entitled, *Love, Acceptance, and Forgiveness.* In it I shared how Christians could become the body of Christ in their communities by practicing real love, acceptance, and forgiveness toward others.

I consider *Monday Morning Church* a sequel. It elaborates upon the principles in that first book and gives them a firm biblical context. In the opening chapters that follow, I deal with the huge implications of Colossians 1:27: "Christ in you, the hope of glory." I also suggest the ultimate Jesus Question that the church, as Christ's body, must pose to a secular, godless, and hurting world: "Is there anything I can do for you?"

In the rest of the book, I describe how we, as Spirit-filled people, are equipped and deployed by Christ to be the church on Monday. I believe that understanding this equipping and deployment will produce confidence, courage, and a renewed trust in God and his work in us. In fact, I almost titled this sequel, *Confidence, Courage, and Trust.* Just as love, acceptance, and forgiveness must be the hallmark of how we live and what we do in the world, so confidence, courage, and trust must be the very fiber of who we are.

Love, acceptance, and forgiveness without confidence, courage, and trust can become passive and idealistic. Confidence, courage, and trust without love, acceptance, and forgiveness can lead to arrogance and pride. But put them together and release them into a fallen, godless culture, and the very person, life, and redemptive power of Christ is unleashed!

As you will see, I have chosen to work out the concepts in this book through a study of Paul's letter to the Ephesians. I've found that preaching and teaching from Ephesians, without fail, builds confidence, courage, and trust in individual Christians. It redefines our very understanding of Christian-ness!

This book is not a commentary, however. Rather, my intent is to use Paul's message as an illustration and dramatic guide to becoming the church on Monday. If we listen carefully, this little letter, written so long ago, will tell us in clear and unequivocal terms who we are, what we have, and how we are to live in order to accomplish the phenomenal task of being the resident presence of Christ on earth.

Evangelism as a primary goal is often artificial and powerless. But when it's a serendipity of Spirit-filled believers being Jesus in their world, it is natural and unstoppable. It's my fervent prayer that this book will sharpen our hearing, expand our understanding, and release us confidently, courageously, and in full trust to be Jesus to the world around us. May you and I, together, become the church on Monday!

The
RADICAL
RELOCATION
of
GOD

You are called not so much to do great things, as to be a great person—and that person is Jesus Christ. The church of Jesus Christ is the resident presence of Jesus in the world. That's a foundational principle of incarnational Christianity.

I remember when the Lord began to nudge me about becoming a pastor. I was in my late teens, and I didn't want anything to do with the ministry. I wanted to be a doctor, because a doctor could make money and also take care of people. Those two things, in that order, were important to me. Interestingly, the Lord didn't seem to care about my plan all that much, even though I explained it to him numerous times.

The reason I didn't want to go into pastoral ministry wasn't because I had something against God or the ministry; it was that my concept of the church and church life was warped. In my young mind, a pastor was the director of religious activities. He put the meetings together and invited people to come and participate. The good pastors did it well, and the poor ones flunked. I didn't want to be an activities director for anything—religious or otherwise.

Still, there was an awareness deep within me that if I were to really follow the intentions of the Lord for my life, I would end up in pastoral ministry, regardless of anything else I might try to pursue. During my university and seminary training, I still carried this ambivalence. I knew being a pastor was what God wanted me to do, but I didn't like the idea.

> The church is not an activities list . . . the church is people!

Our seminary held a chapel service once each week. Along with the many scholars who spoke during those services, one distinguished pastor always visited once or twice a year. His name was Dr. Richard Halverson, and he was pastor of a large Presbyterian church in Washington, D.C. For many years he was also the chaplain of the United States Senate. A deeply godly man, he always spoke life to our hearts. Scholars from all over the world gave us theological treatises, few of which we could understand. As proper seminarians we tried to appear intelligent and interested. But when Dr. Halverson came, we felt as if Jesus were speaking to us.

After one of these services, some of us were having coffee in the cafeteria when Dr. Halverson joined us and began a conversation. One of the students asked, "Dr. Halverson, where is your church?" This seemed like a perfectly reasonable question to me, but Dr. Halverson looked quite perplexed and hesitated to answer. Then he glanced at his watch.

"Well, it's three o'clock in Washington, D.C. The church I

pastor is all over the city. It's driving buses, serving meals in restaurants, sitting in board meetings, having discussions in the Pentagon, deliberating in the Congress." He knew exactly where his church was, and he went on and on with his lengthy listing. Then he added, "Periodically, we get together at a building on Fourth Street, but we don't spend much time there. We're mostly in the city."

A bomb went off in my head. All of my out-of-joint ideas about the church suddenly snapped into place. I heard that the church is not an activities list. It's not a series of things people do. The church is people! If it were simply a series of activities—well, I already had plenty of things to do in my life. But if the church, in fact, is people, then I could be interested—even excited!

It was a wonderful revelation. It presented something to which I could give my life. Because to me, people are very important. I love people.

My wife was putting me through seminary by teaching school. When she came home that day, I announced, "Honey, I found out what the church is!"

"Well, that's good," she replied, "since in about six months we'll be pastoring one."

Excitedly, I recounted the conversation with Dr. Halverson, and she got excited with me. What would happen if we took seriously the concept that the church is people—people in whom Jesus really does dwell?

We began discussing and exploring the idea. All kinds of scriptures began to fall into place. For instance, "The church, which is his body, the fullness of him who fills everything in every way" (Ephesians 1:22–23). That's a bombshell of a verse! The church—the fullness of Jesus? If that's true, then it has incredible implications for those of us who make up the body of Christ!

Then there's Colossians 1:26–27. Paul mentions a mystery, a secret, that God kept so well, no one even knew he had a secret! Paul wrote, "The mystery . . . has been kept hidden for ages and generations, but is now disclosed to the saints. To them God has chosen to make known among the Gentiles the glorious riches of this mystery, which is *Christ in you, the hope of glory*."

If you think of the church in terms of activities, then these verses make no sense. They're just religious simile; figures of speech. But what if the church is people and God really indwells these people? Then these verses are profound. They captured my attention back in seminary. They still hold it firmly today. In fact, it is the pursuit of this concept that has been and still is the focus of my life—this matter, this experiment, of Christians being Jesus in our world.

Often people think of God as distant, "out there." We sing to the God out there, imploring him to come here. We go to God's house and beg him in religious tones to join us. Where does he come from? Where does he go when we leave? Does he hang around empty buildings, hoping we'll come back and see him sometime?

If Colossians 1 is true and Christ really is in us—well, that changes everything! If "Christ in you, the hope of glory" defines actual reality, our perception of God, the church, and ourselves, as believers, must change. The implications are astounding. And the first implication is this: there has been a radical relocation of the expressive presence of God.

Chapter 1: The RADICAL RELOCATION of GOD

Stage 1: God Out There

As we go back through history, we can see this radical relocation taking place in three stages.

Stage 1 is recounted in the Old Testament. The God-out-there begins to act into our reality. He comes *upon* the sacrifices; he comes *upon* the prophets; he comes *upon* the mountain. He has to act into our reality, because we have separated ourselves from him. It's not that he moved away from us; it's that we chose to live without him. Now he begins to reestablish his presence in a way we will be able to understand and respond to.

Our very lives depend on his succeeding. When we chose to live without him, we didn't know we'd made a fatal step. We didn't understand that our life source is not biological only; our life source is spiritual. After God formed man out of the dust of the earth, he, then, did what had not been done before in all his creative activity: he "breathed into his nostrils the breath of life" (Genesis 2:7). The word *breathed* can be translated *kissed*. This man, this human being, this living soul, was alive, not simply because of biology. His life was based on an intimate relationship with God.

It is the same for all of us. When that intimacy is broken, the soul dies. We didn't understand this. But now God begins to act into our reality in order to reestablish this life-support system of an intimate relationship with himself. He begins acting from out there to come to us here.

I have to admit, when I consider this God of the Old Testament, he seems pretty austere, severe, unpredictable, even frightening. I mean, think of the story in Numbers 16. The sons of Korah and their families were wiped out in the wake of his anger, when the

15

ground opened up and swallowed them after they'd complained and rebelled against Moses and Aaron. (I'm glad God no longer swallows complainers. That would thin out the church ranks real fast.)

Frankly, he bothers me. He feels a little arbitrary; makes me nervous. He knows too much and has too much power. The children of Israel believed if you saw this God face-to-face, you would die. He was held in such awe that they would not even pronounce his name.

The God of the Old Testament establishes the fact of his reality and his holiness, but he also establishes the fact of our vulnerability. There's something deeply and fatally wrong with us. We know there is a God, and we know we are in some way responsible to him; but we can't seem to fulfill that responsibility. To appease him, we take our lambs or our turtledoves and offer a sacrifice. The high priest spills the blood and says a prayer, but we walk away from the altar the exact same people we were when we came. What a terrifying state to be in—aware of the wide abyss between us and the God-out-there, but unable to do anything to close the gap!

Some time ago a popular song announced that God is watching us from a distance. That's not a comforting view. If there is a God and the best he can do is sit out there and watch us, we don't have a loving God on our hands; we have a sadistic monster. If he can sit and watch the horror and terror and bloodshed and suffering of humanity and do nothing, he's not the kind of God who can do us any good. Our pain is too deep, our hopelessness too real. A God who watches from a distance is a mockery.

But God is not a mockery. Through the ways and words of

this God of the Old Testament, we are given an unfolding revelation; an ongoing, progressive revealing of his person. His law is like a schoolmaster bringing us to Christ (see Galatians 3:24). The God-out-there begins to reveal his character. He becomes clearer; we gain understanding as we go.

Nevertheless, we eventually come to an impasse. By the end of the Old Testament, we understand there is still a huge gap between us and God, a gap we cannot possibly bridge. We can't go to him; he's beyond our reach. Unless this austere God-out-there actually steps over the gap and into our world, we have no hope.

Stage 2: Emmanuel—God with Us

When we think about this type of God coming to be with us, it's not particularly good news. If he's coming to town today, I'll leave until tomorrow, thank you, and you can tell me how it went! We don't really want to meet him. It's not that we don't like him; we're afraid that he won't like *us*.

How can he come to us in a way that doesn't terrify us, in a way that doesn't cause us to run and hide? How can he step into our world and our lives at a nonthreatening, intimate level?

Doesn't he choose a remarkable way? He simply slips into a little nothing town called Bethlehem as *a baby*. No one is intimidated by a baby. We hold this infant in our arms, bounce him on our knees. We don't know we're holding God; we have no idea. He takes our hearts. Then he grows up. He lives with us for thirty years, and we don't know he is God. We think he is a carpenter. We buy tables and chairs from him.

"Where'd you get that table?"

"In Nazareth—that carpenter made it."

"Joseph?"

"No, the kid, Jesus."

"Incredible table. A real artist."

Of course it's an incredible work of art. *God* made the table! But we don't know he is God. He is one of us.

God Isn't Angry

When we do find out that Jesus is God, we're shocked. He isn't the way gods are supposed to be. He is very different. In fact, the first thing we notice is that he isn't mad at anybody.

Of course, before this moment, we had written the book on God based on a God-out-there. You get wrong ideas about a God who is separate. You don't understand what he's really like. When we wrote the book on God, he was angry, because we dressed him in clothes like ours. If there was a God and he knew people like us, he'd be pretty upset, right? So all our mythologies included an angry God—if not enraged, then disgusted, unpleasant, insensitive; a God who had to be appeased. We developed elaborate systems to accomplish a tenuous safety.

I'm shocked at how many people—even Christians—are still trying to love a God they're convinced is angry or out to get them. They blame the difficulties of their lives on a God who's punishing them. They don't really know who God is.

That's why Jesus comes—to reveal God fully. As Jesus steps into our reality, God himself steps into three dimensions. "Anyone who has seen me has seen the Father," Jesus says (John 14:9). Of course, we can't see all of God; our perception is restricted by time and space. But what we do see is accurately and fully God. Jesus is fully representative of who God is. That means if Jesus is not angry with us, then there is no God out there who is. *There is no angry God out there.* That's quite a revelation!

God Doesn't Condemn Us

Not only is Jesus not angry, but some of the things he says are very ungodlike. For instance, he says, "I have not come to condemn you." That's a strange statement in the mouth of God. We're certainly sinful, and he is certainly holy. There is plenty of room for condemnation.

That's why the story of the woman caught in adultery is so amazing to me (John 8:3–11). What is going on inside her as she lies there in the middle of the street, the leaders of the city standing around her and proclaiming that she deserves to die? To them she is nothing more than a piece of garbage to be disposed of. What would happen inside *you* if you heard yourself described that way—if you were the object of such derision and obscene ridicule?

They declare, "Jesus, our religious law says adulterers should be killed. What do you say?"

"You're right, let's kill her," Jesus replies. "The one of you without sin, you begin the execution. You throw the first stone." Then he bends over and writes something in the sand.

I've heard sermons and theories about what Jesus wrote; frankly, we haven't got a clue. (I have a friend who thinks he was writing the names of the woman's accusers and the dates they had visited her. I don't know; it's a compelling theory, isn't it?) All we know for sure is when Jesus looks up, the city leaders are gone.

Now the woman is left with the one person who *could* throw the rock, the one person without sin. Without a doubt, this is her unlucky day. What a vulnerable position to be in—alone with God in your sin!

At this point in the story, I can't help but wonder: *How is Jesus going to deal with this woman?* I consider myself a pretty loving person; but if I were Jesus, I would certainly moralize a little. Obviously, there's a direct connection between the mess she's in and the life she's lived. Sometimes it's helpful to draw attention to such connections. *How is Jesus going to take advantage of this teaching moment?*

> You can either condemn or give life, but you can't condemn and give life.

To my astonishment, he doesn't! Instead, he asks her, "Where are your accusers? Doesn't anyone condemn you?"

She replies, "No, my Lord," and you can almost hear the unspoken words that surely followed: "What are *you* going to do?"

That's when Jesus makes this remarkable statement: "Neither do I condemn you. Now go, and don't sin anymore." He doesn't bring up her past. He doesn't mention her lifestyle. He makes no commentary of any kind on her condition.

You're missing a great opportunity here, Jesus! You've got a ready-made audience. Forgive her, but make her pay a little. Make your point.

He didn't make his point, and he never does make his point in a condemning way. Instead, he says, "I haven't come to condemn you."

Incredible! God comes into the world, and he doesn't condemn us. My question is, *Why not? We're surely condemnable, and you're a holy God. If you haven't come to condemn us, why have you come? What are you doing here?*

His answer is too good to be true: "I have come to give you life" (see John 10:10). You see, you can either condemn *or* give life, but you can't condemn *and* give life. You can't do both; you must choose one or the other. If Jesus were to choose to condemn us, we would have no hope. But he chooses to give us life.

The Jesus Question

Another curious thing Jesus says is this: "I did not come to be served" (see Mark 10:45). That's very ungodlike. The way we wrote the book, gods are for serving. If you serve them well, they'll be nice to you—most of the time. If you don't serve them well, they'll get you. Sometimes even if you do serve them well, they'll get you! But the order is clear: we serve them; they don't serve us.

Yet here is Jesus Christ stepping out of eternity to reveal the only God there is, and he says, "I haven't come to be served." Now to me that doesn't make sense. Again, my question is, *If you haven't come to be served, why are you here? Why did you come?*

And again, his answer is amazing: "I haven't come to be served, but to serve."

Immediately I begin to recall all the questions Jesus asked throughout the Gospels. Almost always they came down to this: "What can I do for you?" What were his first words to blind Bartimaeus? "What would you like to have me do for you?" What about the lepers? "What can I do for you?" What about the man at the pool? "What can I do for *you*?"

I call it the Jesus Question. It's simply this: "Is there anything in your life about which only God can do something?" Jesus has come to ask that question. Not to condemn us, not to set us straight, not to deepen our guilt, not to make a point, but to ask a simple question: "Can I do anything for you?"

Now, if I were to ask you, "Is there anything I can do for you?" it wouldn't be rhetorical; I would mean it. I would want to help. But we would quickly come to the point where I'd have to admit, "I really would love to, but I can't do that. I'm at the end of my resources."

But what if Jesus were standing in front of you asking the same question? It's an entirely different question, isn't it? There are things only God can do for us. He has come to make his resources available to us in the midst of our hopelessness.

To me, it's almost beyond belief that God would come to us not in anger, not to condemn us, but to give us life and ask this question, this Jesus Question. That's what stage 2 is all about: Emmanuel. God with us. God asking, "What can I do for you?"

My thought is, *What could be better?* But it does get better. There is still a third stage in the radical relocation of God.

A WINDOW in TIME

The last conversation Jesus had with his disciples is fascinating—even amusing, from our vantage point in history. By combining the accounts in Luke 24 and Acts 1, we can assume it went something like this:

Jesus is standing on a hill called the Mount of Ascension. "Fellas, I'm leaving," he announces.

They say: "Where are you going?"

He replies, "Well, you can't come."

They ask, "So what should we do?"

He answers: "Go back to Jerusalem."

"What should we do there?"

"Well, just hang out."

"How long should we stay there?"

"Until the promise of the Father comes."

"Uh, what's that?"

"You'll know it when it arrives."

Part 1: WHERE IS GOD ON MONDAY?

"How long should we wait?"

"Just stay there until it comes."

"Well, what should we do then?"

"Do what you're told."

"Is that it?"

"Basically, yes."

"Is there anything else?"

"No, not really."

And while he's speaking, he begins lifting up off the ground.

Now, we don't do much of that where I come from. Personally, I don't want people floating off in the middle of a conversation. If I'm talking to you, stay on the ground! We read so many of the stories in the Bible as if everything that happens is expected and normal. The fact is, the disciples really hadn't seen much of that kind of thing either. A person lifting off the ground wasn't something that happened every day in first-century Israel.

So here they are, watching Jesus, and you can be sure they are as dumbfounded as you and I would be. In fact, the Scripture says that as Jesus goes out of sight, they are standing there looking up; the exact biblical phrase in Acts 1:10 means "gaping openmouthed into heaven." I can understand that. I certainly would stand there "gaping openmouthed into heaven" too.

But angels see that sort of thing all the time; it's no big deal to them. So they come and ask, "What are you looking at? Go on and do what Jesus said."

"Well, he really didn't tell us to do anything."

"Then just go on back to Jerusalem and hang out."

So the disciples return to Jerusalem and hang out. What else can they do?

Stage 3: God in Us

One day, when they are all together in an upper room, they hear a loud noise—something like the approach of a really big storm. Dr. Luke, an eyewitness, wrote later that it sounded like a "rushing mighty wind" (Acts 2:2 NKJV). But they look out the windows, and the trees aren't moving; dust isn't flying. When they realize this isn't a natural phenomenon but rather a supernatural one, each person immediately understands something very profound is happening. Their history suddenly explodes into the present.

This "rushing mighty wind," they know, represents the presence of the God of their forefathers, Abraham, Isaac, and Jacob. Hundreds of years earlier, when God brought the Israelites out of Egypt, the Egyptian armies pursued their Jewish slaves to the edge of the Red Sea—an apparent dead end. But then Moses took a stick, reached out over the sea, and said a prayer. The people went back into their tents, and a "rushing mighty wind" blew all night. When the Israelites awoke in the morning, the sea was parted, and they crossed on a freeway. They were saved by the wind, which graphically depicted the supernatural presence of God.

These 120 people gathered in the upper room knew the Exodus story well; they've heard it repeated over and over since childhood. Now *they're* the ones experiencing the "rushing mighty wind." (The Greek phrase for the wind in Acts 2:2 is the equivalent of the Hebrew phrase in Exodus 14:21.) Surely something remarkable is happening. Is this the "promise" Jesus told them to wait for?

If there is any doubt, the next symbol makes it crystal clear: fire appears in the room, yet the room is not on fire. When we think back to what happened that day, we often assume fire simply appeared on the people's heads; but if you read the grammar and text closely, it's clear what appeared first was a ball of fire in the center of the room.

Again, for the disciples, history leaps off the page. Throughout the Old Testament, fire stood for God's supernatural presence: the fire on the mountain, the fire that consumed the sacrifice, the pillar of fire by night. And now the fire is in the upper room! There can be no mistake. The disciples know they're in the supernatural presence of God—the God whose name their people will not pronounce, in whose presence they think they will surely die.

God is in the room with them—and, yet, they feel no terror, no fear, no panic. Why? Because, in the person of Jesus, God had walked with them for three-and-a-half years. He was not unknown; he was not the God-out-there. Through Jesus, he had been fully revealed to them. He had become Emmanuel, the God with us.

Then the most remarkable thing happens. No wonder Jesus's last earthly conversation with them had been so short and lacking in detail! Jesus knew they'd have no frame of reference for understanding what was about to take place.

From the single ball of fire, little flames (Acts 2:3 calls them "tongues of fire") begin to peel off and come to rest on the heads of each of the 120 people in the room. There is no longer a central fire; it has dispersed, and the fire is on each individual. Where is the God of Abraham, Isaac, and Jacob now? He is not just *with* them. He is *in* them. *God has come to dwell in them!*

Now, suddenly, the strange words Jesus spoke to them at the Last Supper make sense: "He lives with you and will be in you" (John 14:17). And the words before his ascension? When Jesus told them to wait for "the promise of the Father," he didn't mean a promise the Father was making to them; he meant the promise of *the Father*. There is now a unique residency of God in each of them. The intimate relationship between God and man, broken so long ago, has been reestablished!

It all begins to come together: Stage 1 was "God out there." It was what their ancestors had known. Stage 2 was "God with us." It was what the disciples had come to understand as they walked with Jesus those three-and-a-half years. Now, in the upper room, they are ushered into the most amazing stage of all—Stage 3: "God in us."

> **Through Jesus, God had become Emmanuel, the God with us.**

When the profundity of what has just happened sinks in, their reaction is far from fear. They begin to rejoice! "Can it really be true?" "Is God really *in* us?" In fact, they get so carried away with joy, the people on the street think they're having a party. *They must be drinking,* the people assume. *After all, no one gets as happy as they sound without a little artificial help.*

Then again, they reason, as they hear the disciples continue in their revelry, *the bars haven't been open long enough for anyone to get that happy.* So they draw closer, curious to find out what's going on.

Peter stands up to explain. He reaches back eight hundred years into Israel's history and picks out as his text four verses from the little book of Joel.

Now, the book of Joel is about grasshoppers—big grasshoppers called locusts—that had overrun the country, absolutely devastating everything in their path. By the time the locusts were done, the countryside looked as if a fire had swept through it.

We don't know much about Joel. We don't know where he came from or where he went. The book of Joel is his only recorded sermon, and it takes up only three chapters. Apparently, Joel stepped out on the stage of time, delivered his message, and left. And his message was basically this: if you think this plague of locusts was bad, wait till the day of the Lord comes. That's the book of Joel.

It's a pretty simple message—except for a few statements Joel dropped about two-thirds of the way into it. For eight hundred years those statements were left hanging, suspended in Jewish history. If Jewish literature referred to them at all, it was to say, "We don't know what they mean yet." For eight long centuries they remained a mystery.

But now Peter reaches back, picks up those verses, and declares, "This is what was spoken by the prophet Joel: 'In the last days, God says, I will pour out my Spirit on all people.'" Then he continues quoting those remarkable verses recorded in Acts 2:17–21:

> "Your sons and daughters will prophesy,
>> your young men will see visions,
>> your old men will dream dreams.
> Even on my servants, both men and women,
>> I will pour out my Spirit in those days,
>>> and they will prophesy.
> I will show wonders in the heaven above
>> and signs on the earth below,
>> blood and fire and billows of smoke.

The sun will be turned to darkness and the moon to blood
before the coming of the great and glorious day
of the Lord.
And everyone who calls on the name of the Lord will be
saved."

What an incredible statement! And what a perfect fit with what the disciples had just experienced!

The Last Days

Something was born on that day of Pentecost—something called "the last days." Joel said, "In *the last days* these things will happen." What the disciples experienced in the upper room was the beginning of the last days.

We know from Scripture, then, when the last days began. We also know the last days will end. We just don't know *when* they will end—only that "the great and glorious day of the Lord" will forever close the last days window.

So what we have is this: a specific period of time determined by God, with a distinct beginning and a distinct, although undisclosed, ending. Within this time frame, God has a profound purpose. From Joel's prophetic message, we know this purpose works out through three continuing events—things that never happened on our planet before and will never happen again:

1. A Prophetic Community Is Formed

Before that day in the upper room, there were prophets, and there were schools of the prophets; but there had never been a general community of prophetic people. Pentecost changed that.

What do prophets do? Consistently throughout Scripture, prophets do three things. They do them at different times and in different ways, but they basically do the same three things: they see, hear, and speak from God's perspective. They bring God's perspective into our human reality.

Now, in the last days, there is a community of people—men, women, girls, and boys—all of whom are capable of practicing these three prophetic things, wherever they are. They are not specialists upon whom the Spirit occasionally comes. They are people who live in prophetic awareness, *because God is in them*. As a result, God's perspective is available at all times, at every stage and level of life, throughout the population of the planet.

2. The World Falls Apart

Joel said that in the last days, signs such as blood, fire, and smoke would appear in the heavens and on the earth. Biblically, these signs represent the world as we know it falling apart.

3. People Call on the Lord

The third thing that happens in the last days is that "everyone who calls on the name of the Lord will be saved."

Let me ask you a question: when do people tend to call on the name of the Lord to be saved? Often it is when their world is falling apart. Have you ever been with anybody whose world is falling apart? Did he or she call on the name of the Lord? I've observed people call on the name of the Lord in one of two ways, and occasionally both: Sometimes they pray and sometimes they curse. Sometimes they curse and pray. All they know is their world is coming apart at the seams. They hurt in places they didn't know could hurt, and they don't know what to do about it. They know they need help—not some kind of general help, but something deeper, something more.

May I suggest something to you? *These* are the last days; *we* are that prophetic community; and it is *our world* that is falling apart. The reason we're here at this specific point in history is to bring God's perspective into the world's devastation and respond when people call on the Lord to be saved.

I'm convinced that as Christians we're not about programs. We're not about bigger or better blessings. We're about responding to people who call for help because their world is falling apart. These individuals aren't looking to be converted—they're looking for help! Being their help—by being the presence of Christ in their lives—is the *only* thing we're about. Everything else we do is secondary and can even detour us from carrying out the true purpose of the church.

Responding to the Call

Let's make up a story. Let's say you're at work, on a coffee break. As you stand there in the lounge pouring your coffee, one of your colleagues joins you. You greet him and ask how he's doing. Out of the blue he begins telling you about the night before.

"You know, I think last night was about the worst night of my life."

"Why?" you respond. "What happened?"

"My son is seventeen, a very responsible kid," he says. "He asked to use the car and went out with his friends. Usually, if he's going to be late, he calls and lets us know when he'll be home. But last night it was past midnight and he hadn't called, so we got concerned. Finally the phone rang at 2:00 a.m. My wife and I were frantic; we were afraid to answer it. I picked up the phone, and there was a policeman on the other end. He gave a name and asked if that was my son. I said yes, but I was afraid for him to go on. I didn't know if my boy was dead or what.

"The policeman said, 'I'm sorry to inform you that your son has been involved in a crime with another boy. We've arrested him, and he's in the city jail. You can come down and we'll release him to your custody, but he'll have to come back for a trial. It's a serious situation.'

> You simply ask, "Is there anything I can do for you?"

"I couldn't believe it. My son's never been in trouble; it was the furthest thing from my mind. My wife and I drove down to the police station. We didn't even know what to say to each other. They brought my son out in handcuffs. Our eyes met, and I didn't know what to do. They took the handcuffs off, and we got in the car and drove home. I'm still stunned. It just feels like my whole world is disintegrating around me."

Why is he telling *you* this? You don't know him—at least not *this* well. Other people overhear snatches of the conversation and understand this man is having trouble with his son. But you, you're not just "other people." You're a prophetic person in whom Jesus Christ himself lives. You're hearing what Jesus would hear if he were standing there. That's why this man is talking to you.

This man is calling on the name of the Lord. He doesn't know it, but Jesus knows. Jesus doesn't want him to be alone when his world begins falling apart. That's why you're there. Perhaps the only reason you've had this job for the last five years is so you'd be there having coffee on the morning this father's world begins to crumble.

How do you respond to this man? What do you do? That's the important question now. Give him your pastor's card and tell him to call the church office? Invite him to the service on Sunday? It's a crucial moment, isn't it?

I'd like to suggest that those kinds of encounters are happening all over every city—including yours and mine. Very often we don't recognize what's going on; or we recognize it, but we don't have a clue what to do. A response is so simple. But we've taken fifteen weeks of classes on how to win souls; we've memorized hundreds of scriptures that we don't know how to apply. If people so much as blink religiously, we try to jam it all down their throats. We try to get them converted. But is evangelistic technique what's needed here?

Let me ask you a simple question: if Jesus were standing there, what would he do? What *did* he do when he was faced with the catastrophic in people's lives? When he was approached by people whose lives were coming apart? What did he say? What was his question?

"Is there anything I can do for you?"

That's all you do: you ask the Jesus Question. It doesn't take fifteen weeks of advanced Bible study to do it. You don't have to be a Christian for fifteen years first. You don't have to have all your problems solved.

You simply ask, "Is there anything I can do for you?" This is the question that releases the life and ministry and gifts of the Holy Spirit into your everyday world. "Christ in *you*, the hope of glory." *You* are filled with the Holy Spirit. That means Jesus is present. And that means when you ask the Jesus Question, you are fully equipped and capable of responding exactly the way Jesus would.

The gifts of the Holy Spirit were designed for the street, for moments like this. They weren't given so that Christians can work them on each other. The gifts of the Spirit are how Jesus works through you to touch the lives of hurting people.

Let's go back to our story. After listening to your colleague and recognizing the prophetic significance of what is going on, you begin to respond.

"You know, I have a son too," you say, "and I can only imagine how I'd feel if I got that phone call. Is there anything I can do for you?"

Maybe you wouldn't use those exact words; that's OK. Respond in the way that's natural to you. Everyone listening to this man's story would respond differently to the situation; that's why the Holy Spirit has *you* there. He wants it done the way *you* would do it. If you get nervous and try to follow a formula, you're going to blow the whole thing. Don't get religious—just relax and respond the way you'd naturally respond to a hurting person.

Let's imagine further. "Well, you know, my wife and I don't have many friends," your colleague says. "We both work, and we were thinking last night, 'Man, we'd sure like to have someone to talk to.' I don't want to impose on you, but maybe it would help if we could have a cup of coffee together tonight and talk."

Don't you dare say, "It's Wednesday night, and I have to go to Bible study"! This is what Bible study is about, right here—this is it!

Chapter 2: A WINDOW in TIME

If all our activities don't serve encounters like this, then they're a colossal waste of time. Being a Christian isn't about programs—how big and how many and how much and how great. It isn't about position or power or getting blessed. There's an eternity in heaven to be blessed, and we'll have plenty of time to enjoy it.

Our time here is about being Jesus in our world. Jesus didn't come to our planet on vacation; he came on assignment. Likewise, you and I have not been born into these last days accidentally. There's divine strategy at work. We don't just happen to be where we are, bumping into people whose worlds are falling apart. God placed us here on purpose.

I don't believe in fatalism, but I do believe in destiny—and we are people of destiny. Remember, you have been redeemed by the blood of the Lamb. You are filled with the Spirit of God. You are living in this window in time called the last days. You are where you are because God strategically placed you there.

The question is, Are you open for business?

Part 2

WHO YOU ARE

Where
CONFIDENCE
BEGINS

As you have probably gathered by now, to me, Monday is the most important day of the week. Monday is the day when Jesus enters our world. I'm not talking about believers standing on street corners preaching or passing out religious tracts. I'm talking about Jesus in you and in me, expressing his life to the people around us as we live our everyday lives.

Most of the time when we think of church, we think of Sunday. But Sunday is really about Monday. If our job as Christians was simply to gather together and worship God, we could do that in heaven. But our job is more than that; that's why God has us strategically placed right where we are.

What is our job exactly? This may surprise you, but it's not to convert people. Scripture says very little about us converting people. What it does say is this: "You will be my witnesses" (Acts 1:8). In other words, we will be illustrations—living proof—that Jesus Christ was, in fact, God, and he is still alive. We do that through the process of being people not only in whom Christ lives, but through whom Christ expresses himself in our individual worlds.

I have suggested several times now that our primary goal is not converting people to Christianity. Let me explain what I mean. It is unquestionably important that people make a decision to follow Christ; that they turn to him, invite him into their lives, and experience his forgiveness and cleansing for their sin. But I see this "turning" as a result, not a goal.

Jesus said plainly, "[I] came to seek and to save what was lost" (Luke 19:10). Our job is to continue that mission—not to capture and convert, but to bring Christ's presence into a lost world and make his power and love available. Some may reject his offer of love and help. Others may accept it and go on their way. Still others will choose to turn and follow him.

Remember, not everyone Jesus ministered to chose to follow. Where were the crowds he fed, the multitudes he healed, at the time of his death? Many of them were standing beneath the cross spitting and shouting, "Crucify him!" The fact is, after three-and-a-half years of public ministry, Jesus left behind only 120 followers in a borrowed room.

Now it's up to us to minister as he did—with no hooks. Of course, we want to influence people to follow Christ. But we must bring his healing to people, because people hurt. We must bring his hope, because people are hopeless. We must bring his love, because people are bereft of unconditional love. We must do all these things without ulterior motive. People may respond or they may not—just as they did two thousand years ago.

Ephesians: The Manual for Church Life

The part of the Bible I love more than any other is the book of Ephesians. I frequently find myself going back there, preaching and pastoring from its wisdom. If you want a lifetime memory project, memorize Ephesians! Its message is fundamental to our understanding of what it means to be Christian—what it means to be the body of Christ in our world. It tells us how to be the church on Monday. I call it the manual for church life. Here's a simple outline:

- The first two chapters of Ephesians deal with the formation of the church—in other words, how the church came to be and who the church is.

- Chapter 3 lays out the purpose of the church.

- Half of chapter 4 describes the preparation and ministry of the church.

- The rest of the letter concerns the lifestyle of the church.

The *church*, as I'm using the word and as Paul uses it in Ephesians, is not an institution or organization to which we go or belong. When you ask, "Where is the church?" I can't answer with an address (as Dr. Halverson taught me), because the church is not a location and never has been. Nor is the church defined anywhere in Scripture in institutional terms.

The "institution" referred to in Scripture is Judaism; and when Jesus came, the Jewish religious system was made obsolete. That institution could bring us to an understanding of our need for Christ, but it could take us no further. When Jesus came, he transcended the institution.

So when I say *church*, please don't picture an organization or a set of religious programs. Don't picture a pastor and a church board, meetings on Sunday and home groups on Wednesday. Those are things the church may do, but they are not the church.

No, the church is *people*. What kind of people? People in whom Jesus Christ lives and expresses himself. People redeemed through the blood of Christ. People in whom the Holy Spirit has come to live. People through whom the Spirit is ministering. As the book of Ephesians makes clear, the church is not just people *experiencing* Jesus; the church is people *expressing* Jesus.

The forms we use to organize ourselves are not the issue in Ephesians. It matters very little how our churches are organized. In fact, I doubt God cares, as long as our systems are legal and ethical and release the church on Monday.

> **We don't have a product to push; we have a person to reveal.**

When we think institutionally, we tend to think in sales terms. We think of developing a product. But when we adopt a "sell the church" mode, radical damage is done to the essential purpose and message of the church. It is always a mistake to try to market the church, gloss it up, and sell it. We're not in the sales business. We don't have a product to push; we have a person to reveal. Persons are revealed by persons, not by marketing strategies.

When God chose to reveal himself to our world, he didn't send an angel with a message or a program or a preferred institutional structure. He sent Jesus. The Word, the message he had for us, was Jesus, bound not in leather, but skin; not to be read and put aside, but experienced. A message in flesh and blood—God

42

walking off the page, walking out of all the religious trappings that sought to confine him, and walking right into the lives of those of us who needed him but didn't know it. The forms, the rituals, the elaborate structures—we could never find him there. So he wrapped himself in skin and came looking for us.

That is still his mode of operation. The Father is still revealed, only through flesh and blood. Only through people—people in whom his Spirit lives and through whom his heart reaches.

You are the church. *You* are the revelation of Jesus. *You* are the way others can know him. And so am I.

Our True Identity

Why am I so adamant on this point? Because if we're going to be Jesus in our world, we must understand who we are as individuals first. Without the foundation of an accurate understanding of our true identity, we will never have the confidence, courage, and trust to reach out to others with Christ's healing and love.

A small book on my shelf is titled, *Why Am I Afraid to Tell You Who I Am?* The brilliant author, John Powell, posed that question in a classroom.

"Do you want my answer?" queried a student.

"Yes, of course I do," responded Dr. Powell.

"I am afraid to tell you who I am, because if I tell you who I am, you may not like who I am, and it's all that I have."[1]

That student hit the nail right on the head. He got to the heart of most of our confidence problems. Some of us would back up even further to say, "I am afraid to tell *myself* who I really am, because *I* may not be able to face the awful truth." Or even further: "I don't know who I am, and I haven't got a clue how to find out!"

Part 2: WHO YOU ARE

Where do we go to answer the all-important question, "Who am I?" Do we begin with our parents, our heredity, our racial or ethnic background, our skills or talents (or lack thereof)?

What is most basic? Is it our work?

"Who are you anyway?"

"I'm a pastor."

"Well, that could change; then who will you be?"

Following a miserable golf game one rainy Oregon day, I had a conversation with a friend named Sam about his loss of identity. Sam was a remarkable athlete, but he had reached the age where he could no longer play professional football. His contract had not been renewed; he was through. At thirty-two his battered body and his coaches said, "No more!"

"I don't know who I am," he stammered, making no attempt to hold back his tears. "I feel like I've lost everything!"

All his life he'd been an athlete. Who was he now? A nothing? A nobody?

We are not our jobs or our talents, our families or our heredity. We are not the sum total of other people's opinions of us. We are, rather, the sum total of who God says we are.

The early Christians began their answer to the question, "Who are you?" with a simple phrase: *en Christo*. It means "in Christ." Repeatedly throughout the New Testament, and especially in Paul's writings, God uses en Christo to describe who we are as believers. For example, Ephesians 1:1 begins: "Paul, an apostle of Christ Jesus by the will of God, to the saints in Ephesus, the faithful *in Christ Jesus*."

In chapter 1 we talked about the profound meaning of "Christ in you" (Colossians 1:27). If you have invited Jesus

44

Christ into your life, you can be certain he really is there. He is *in you*. (By the way, it's also true that if you have not invited him, he is *not* there. He comes only by invitation. But he always comes when invited.)

Just as profound is this concept of *you in Christ*. What can you know about yourself, if you are in Christ? Here is a list of some of the features of your identity *en Christo*. Right now, as a believer, you are:

- Justified in Christ (Romans 3:24)

- Sanctified in Christ (1 Corinthians 1:2)

- Vindicated in Christ (2 Corinthians 12:19)

- Liberated in Christ (Galatians 2:4)

- Exultant in Christ (Philippians 1:26)

- Complete in Christ (Colossians 2:9–10)

- Gracious in Christ (Philemon 15–16)

- Hopeful in Christ (1 Thessalonians 1:3)

- Strong and faithful in Christ (1 Timothy 1:18–19)

- Triumphant in Christ (2 Corinthians 2:14)

You are all of these things *en Christo*—the result of the covenant God made with mankind through Christ. When Jesus came to earth, he fulfilled the human side of this covenant. Let me explain.

A Covenant Relationship

God has always defined the way in which he and mankind relate to one another through the concept of *covenant*. A covenant sets the parameters for a relationship. In the Old Testament, God established his side of what we now call the Old Covenant. The people of Israel understood that if they kept this covenant—these laws, these rules—then God would respond in certain ways and they would be blessed. David wrote, "I know, O LORD, that your laws are righteous. . . . Your law is my delight" (Psalm 119:75, 77). He understood the value of covenant.

The Benefits of the Law

During a conference in Switzerland, I was speaking about this idea of covenant, and I mentioned that we are expected to love the Law of God. "That sounds strange," I remarked. "Why would you love laws? Of course, you would do your best to keep them, but why would you delight in them?"

After the meeting, a gracious Jewish woman named Stella came to me and asked, "Can we talk?"

Stella was eighty-five years old and obviously well-educated. We proceeded to have a fascinating conversation about the Law and about how she, as a child growing up in a Jewish community, came to understand it.

"The Law? Oh, it's wonderful," she declared.

"What do you mean by that?" I asked.

"Why, the Law shows us that God cared enough about us to establish contact with us; that he desired to have a relationship with us so much, he was willing to come and tell us how it could be done. I think that's wonderful," she repeated.

"Besides this," she continued, "the Law tells us a great deal about the character of God. His laws reveal the kind of person he is. For example, his laws are moral laws; therefore, we know that God is, in fact, a person of morality."

"That's important!" I agreed. "If you're going to have a God, you'd want one who is predictably good."

"The laws of God also have to do with relationships—our relationship with him, with one another, and with the world around us," Stella went on. "So we know God is not only a moral being, but he puts a priority on relationships. Relationships and people are important to him."

Stella was right on all counts. The Law does something else too: it defines the ways we all want to live (or at least the way we want everyone else to live). Think about the Ten Commandments. Not many people would oppose them in principle. They describe the way God has designed us to live, and something in us naturally responds to them. Nor are we surprised when God tells us, "Now, if you keep my laws, you'll be blessed." The lists of covenant blessings in the Old Testament certainly seem fair and just (see Deuteronomy 27–28).

> **That's where we got into deep trouble: we couldn't obey.**

Here's the thing about a covenant though: it has two parties, and each party has a responsibility. Under the covenant God established, God's responsibility was to define his laws for us and then fulfill his promises when we kept them. Our responsibility, as his people, was simply to obey.

And therein lies the catch. That's where we got into deep trouble: we couldn't obey.

Priests and Rituals

Because we couldn't keep our side of the covenant, a system of rituals was inserted into the package to help us maintain a relationship with God—a relationship we really didn't have a right to, given our disobedience. The Old Testament records the instructions given to the Jewish nation about these rituals. With priests acting as official mediators, we could atone for our sins with sacrifices and offerings.

But the ceremonies and sacrifices couldn't help us in a permanent way. We walked away from the altar the same persons we were when we came. Nothing had changed, except an animal had died and blood had been spilled. There was no change inside of us. We still couldn't keep the covenant, no matter how hard we tried. We were hopeless.

Because of our disobedience, the Law, which was intended to be an expression of God's blessing, became a curse instead (see Romans 7:10–12). Why a curse? Because the result of not keeping the laws—not living within the boundaries God has set—is chaos and destruction. It's not that God gets angry and slaps us around. It's that God's laws define the parameters of health and life. When we live outside those parameters, the results are lethal.

Released from the Curse

In Romans 5:19 we read that because of one man's disobedience, sin entered the whole human race. But because of one man's obedience, the righteousness of God has come to us all. What does this mean?

In all of history there have been only two representative human beings: Adam and Jesus. Adam was the first and he sinned. Because he sinned, we all are infected with sin—every single one of us. Jesus was the second representative, and he was obedient to God in every way. At every point where mankind sinned, Jesus obeyed. At every point of our disobedience, he was obedient. When Satan tempted him in the desert, he came through in obedience. Adam came out of his own temptation doomed—remember how readily he ate the fruit in the garden?

Jesus reversed Adam's disobedience and became the one who, through obedience, fulfilled the Law for us. He released us from the curse of the Law by being 100 percent obedient *for us*.

As Christians we're accused of being narrow-minded and intolerant when we say we believe Jesus Christ is the one and only way to God. But he is the exclusive Savior, the only possibility. To believe otherwise is to call Jesus a liar—or pretend he never lived on earth at all! His claims to being the one and only way to God are unequivocally made and clearly spoken, not once, but many times in the Gospels.

Believing him is not intolerance. The simple truth is, he is the one—the only one—who fulfilled the Law for us. Because of his obedience, our part of the covenant has been kept, and we're free from the curse of the Law. In him we can now receive all the covenant blessings of God. Through him—and him alone—we can enter into God's very presence (see Jude 24).

The New Covenant

Now we don't have to try harder to obey the Law; all we must do is believe in Jesus. But do we?

You see, even now, we can't enter God's presence on our own. We know the evil that lies within us, even in our best moments.

If you had to stand before God on the basis of how well you did this month, you'd be pretty frightened, wouldn't you? But Jesus Christ, who had no sin, became "the righteousness of God" for us (2 Corinthians 5:21). He did right what we could never do. Believing in him means trusting that what he did right, he did for us. It means trusting him to be our righteousness, so that, en Christo, we have a relationship with God that would otherwise be impossible.

And what a relationship! This new relationship with God so radically transforms us, the Bible calls it a "new birth" (1 Peter 1:3). Paul says we're a "new creation" in Christ (2 Corinthians 5:17).

There is often confusion on this point. People tend to believe being a Christian means being perfect, having no more sin. They are quick to point out the flaws and sins of supposed Christians, thinking that by doing so, they are exposing hypocrisy or destroying the validity of Christian faith and experience.

In reality, becoming a Christian means simply that we now have an intimate and significant relationship with God. The life-connection that was broken in Adam, which began the death spiral for all humankind, has been reestablished, because Jesus obeyed and fulfilled our side of the covenant. It is this relationship with God that transforms us—not some act of conversion. Conversion is only the beginning. Getting in the car and starting the motor is necessary to taking a trip, but it's not the trip.

When Does Transformation Take Place?

You don't become transformed *before* you enter into the covenant. Being transformed is a part of the blessing of the covenant. Back in the Old Testament, this transformation was prophesied by

Chapter 3: Where **CONFIDENCE BEGINS**

Ezekiel: "I will give you a new heart and put a new spirit in you; I will remove from you your heart of stone and give you a heart of flesh. And I will put my Spirit in you" (Ezekiel 36:26–27). Another Jewish prophet predicted, "I will put my law in their minds and write it on their hearts" (Jeremiah 31:33).

When you became a Christian, you became a new person in Christ Jesus. You began a transformation process—not because of anything you did or could do, but because of what Jesus did for you. He became righteousness for you, opening the door for you to have a life-changing relationship with God.

"Well," you might say. "That lets me off pretty easy."

I'll say it does!

"Maybe I should get knocked around a little bit, suffer a little punishment."

Isn't that the way we think? But that's not how it works. Because of Jesus, you are fully "accepted in the Beloved" (Ephesians 1:6 NKJV). "For it is by grace you have been saved, through faith— and this not from yourselves, it is the gift of God—not by works, so that no one can boast" (Ephesians 2:8–9). Because he came and fulfilled your side of the covenant, you are now an inheritor of all the promises of God.

That's what it means to be "in Christ." "In Christ" is not a religious feeling. It is not an emotional experience. It's entering into the reality of this Christ-event. Jesus said, "This . . . is the new covenant in my blood" (Luke 22:20). What's new about it? It's not that the covenant has been rewritten; it's that it's finally been kept!

God's laws are the same, his expectations are the same, and his promises are the same. But now, because of Christ's obedience—

51

even to the point of death, of becoming a sacrifice—there's a new covenant. The human side of the covenant has been fulfilled. Perfect obedience combined with perfect love combined with God's perfect laws: the three came together to make a new covenant that never existed before. Because you believe that, you have stepped into his obedience. You are en Christo.

Benefits of the New Covenant

Let's take a look at some of the things that are true for you *in Christ* by glancing through the first chapter of Ephesians printed below. I've put *in Christ, in him,* and similar phrases in italics to emphasize the connection between your position in him and your new identity. In just twenty-one verses these phrases are used over a dozen times:

> Paul, an apostle of Christ Jesus by the will of God,
>
> To the saints in Ephesus, the faithful *in Christ Jesus*:
>
> Grace and peace to you from God our Father and the Lord Jesus Christ.
>
> Praise be to the God and Father of our Lord Jesus Christ, who has blessed us in the heavenly realms with every spiritual blessing *in Christ*. For he chose us *in him* before the creation of the world to be holy and blameless in his sight. In love he predestined us to be adopted as his sons *through Jesus Christ*, in accordance with his pleasure and will—to the praise of his glorious grace, which he has freely given us *in the One he loves*. *In him* we have redemption through his blood, the forgiveness of sins, in accordance with the riches of God's grace that he lavished on us with all wisdom and understanding. And he

made known to us the mystery of his will according to his good pleasure, which he purposed *in Christ*, to be put into effect when the times will have reached their fulfillment—to bring all things in heaven and on earth together under one head, even Christ.

In him we were also chosen, having been predestined according to the plan of him who works out everything in conformity with the purpose of his will, in order that we, who were the first to hope *in Christ*, might be for the praise of his glory. And you also were included *in Christ* when you heard the word of truth, the gospel of your salvation. Having believed, you were marked *in him* with a seal, the promised Holy Spirit, who is a deposit guaranteeing our inheritance until the redemption of those who are God's possession—to the praise of his glory.

For this reason, ever since I heard about your faith *in the Lord Jesus* and your love for all the saints, I have not stopped giving thanks for you, remembering you in my prayers. I keep asking that the God of our Lord Jesus Christ, the glorious Father, may give you the Spirit of wisdom and revelation, so that you may know him better. I pray also that the eyes of your heart may be enlightened in order that you may know the hope to which he has called you, the riches of his glorious inheritance in the saints, and his incomparably great power for us who believe. That power is like the working of his mighty strength, which he exerted *in Christ* when he raised him from the dead and seated him at his right hand in the heavenly realms, far above all rule and authority, power and dominion, and every title that can be given, not only in the present age but also in the one to come. And God placed all things under his feet and appointed him to be head over everything for the church, which is his body, the fullness of him who fills everything in every way. (Ephesians 1)

What a description of the blessings and benefits of the New Covenant! Verse 3 alone is enough to knock our socks off: "Praise be to the God and Father of our Lord Jesus Christ, who has blessed us in the heavenly realms with *every spiritual blessing in Christ*." How many blessings is that? Do you realize that right now, at this very moment, you have everything you need to be spiritual? There is absolutely nothing of a spiritual nature that you don't already have. In Christ *all* spiritual blessings are yours!

Notice we're not talking about *material* blessings. Sometimes this verse is distorted to conclude that, because a particular person has more material blessings than others, he or she is more blessed by God. But Jesus was clear when he said, "A man's life does not consist in the abundance of his possessions" (Luke 12:15).

So what are spiritual blessings? They are whatever you need for spiritual development, spiritual life, and spiritual maturity. You see, with your body you contact the world around you. With your soul you contact yourself, your person, your emotions. With your spirit you contact God. Before you were en Christo, the spiritual part of you was separated from God. Your spirit was "dead in your transgressions and sins" (Ephesians 2:1). But now, God has blessed you "in the heavenly realms with every spiritual blessing in Christ." Your spirit has been resurrected. The spiritual side of your life has unlimited potential, because you're drawing your new life from Christ.

Chapter 3: Where CONFIDENCE BEGINS

Understand, "in the heavenly realms" has nothing to do with floating around in the sky. It has everything to do with living in the presence of God. Because you are in Christ, you are now able to live constantly in God's presence, continuously experiencing the freedom and transformation his presence brings.

But there's more! As if "every spiritual blessing" weren't enough, Paul goes on to list at least nine more benefits of your en Christo covenant position. They're all significant features of your new identity in Christ, and they're found in the first fourteen verses of Ephesians. We'll take a look at each of them in the next two chapters.

Will the REAL YOU Please STAND UP?

Johnny was the best football player in our neighborhood. Bigger than the rest of us, faster and more athletic, he was always one of the captains, and his team always won. We all wanted to be chosen by Johnny. Significance came from being on his team.

I was skinny and small, but I was lightning quick, and I could jump high and long—especially when I was scared, which was most of the time I was playing football in the field. And Johnny always picked me. Scared didn't matter. Fast did. I was "somebody." I was on Johnny's team.

God's Choice

In the safety of my office, I often talk with people who feel as if they are outcasts—unaccepted, unacceptable, always the person left out after everyone else has been chosen for the team. If you have ever felt that way, I can honestly and truthfully tell you what I tell the people in my office, "You are God's choice!"

Ephesians 1:4: "For he chose us in him before the creation of the world to be holy and blameless in his sight." Not only are we blessed with every spiritual blessing, as we discussed in the last chapter; we are also chosen. The choice was made before the creation of the world, and the purpose of that choice was for us to be holy and blameless.

That means I'm God's choice and so are you! That's important to know, especially since the significance of a choice is always directly tied to the significance of the person doing the choosing. I'm amazed to think that the most significant person in all the universe has chosen me! Not because I can run fast, but because he loves me. And he has chosen you, too, for exactly the same reason.

He chooses you today and every moment of your life. It's not that he chose you five years ago, and now he's a little disappointed with his choice. He chooses you today, the way you are now, the person you are now. Because of Jesus, the covenant is fulfilled; God's choice is real and binding. There's nothing that can remove you from him. Sin is no longer a barrier, because Christ tore down that barrier.

Please don't misunderstand me. I'm not implying it doesn't matter how you live. Not at all! Rather, I'm pointing out that Jesus has come and done what we could never do—and we receive the benefits. It's called grace.

I don't know about you, but there are some days when I wouldn't choose me. Do you have those kinds of days? There are times when I'm going through certain struggles, and I wouldn't choose me right then; in fact, I'm surprised my wife stays. Barbara is an amazing person because she stays with me. And I'm pretty amazing because I stay with her. We've chosen each other.

Chapter 4: Will the **REAL YOU** Please **STAND UP?**

Together we wrote a book about marriage called *Choosing to Love*. It emphasizes that in every marriage, a time comes when a husband and wife must decide that their commitment stands, whether or not their needs are being satisfactorily "fulfilled" by their partner. They love each other because they *choose* to, not because they *have* to. In a healthy marriage both spouses understand they can live without each other, but they don't want to; they choose not to.

It would be silly for me to believe Barb is such an inept person that she couldn't have a life without me. She's an extremely capable person, and I'm sure at times she thinks (and I might agree) she could have a better life without me. I'm certainly not her only hope for life! Likewise, I could live without her, but I don't want to. I could do it, but I cringe at the thought!

> **Not only are we blessed with every spiritual blessing, we are also chosen.**

Thankfully, we have both made the choice to be together. We've chosen to love each other. This is the woman I will grow old with—it's a choice. "Doesn't sound very romantic," you say? A chosen love is the very foundation of romance and intimacy, and that choice is sealed by a marriage covenant.

It's in this same sense God has chosen you. You're his choice on your good days and on your bad days. I don't get up in the morning and tell Barb, "Well, I think it's going to be a bad day—you'd better divorce me. But tomorrow will be a little better, so why don't we get remarried then?" Not only would that approach be senseless, it would be expensive.

The times when you most disappoint God and everybody else are the times when Jesus's failure to disappoint God stands for you. Because he is accepted, you are accepted in the Beloved. You are still chosen. You still have access to all the benefits of the covenant. You still participate in the transforming process that comes from having Jesus Christ in your life.

A Recipient of Destiny

So far we've looked at two of the benefits found in Ephesians 1 of being en Christo, "in Christ." We talked about the first benefit in chapter 3: the gift of every spiritual blessing. Benefit number two is the knowledge that we are chosen by God. The third benefit is found in Ephesians 1:4–6: "In love he predestined us to be adopted as his sons [and daughters] through Jesus Christ, in accordance with his pleasure and will—to the praise of his glorious grace, which he has freely given us in the One he loves."

You have a destiny. There is a reason for your life. You are not an accident; there is purpose in your living! Understand, your destiny is not tied to the circumstances of your conception—that is, whether you were planned or wanted by your parents. Simply to be born is to be a recipient of destiny.

What is that destiny? Paul announces that one of God's purposes for your life is that you live "for the praise of his glory" (v. 12).

For the Praise of His Glory

I came to Ephesians 1:12 one Sunday during my first year of preaching through Ephesians, and I talked about the joy of living "for the praise of his glory." The next day Carla, a twenty-one-year-old student, was at work at her part-time job. She was a waitress at a riverside restaurant, where yachts tie up and their wealthy occupants come ashore for elegant meals. That particular Monday a group of retired businessmen came in and proceeded to carry on a rather loud and cynical conversation about the state of society in general and the meaninglessness of life in particular. "Even the younger generation," one of them opined, "has no purpose in life."

A second man turned to Carla and asked, "How about you, sweetie? You're a pretty girl; what are you living for?"

Carla smiled, stopped filling the water glasses, and unhesitatingly replied, "I'm living for the praise of God's glory."

"You're what?"

"Say that once again, young lady!"

The businessmen didn't understand about destiny, but Carla did. To have a destiny means there is a destination to our journey in life; we have a direction. We are not aimlessly wandering around. As believers in Christ we are not racing from one accident of fate to another. We are not disconnected parts of a disintegrating whole.

We are, in fact, people of destiny.

I am not referring here to the theological doctrine of predestination. This is not a chapter on man's free will versus God's sovereignty. Ephesians 1 is sometimes used for that particular argument, but not here, not me, not now.

Rather, I am underlining the remarkable and wonderful reality that God has made each of us capable of high purpose. The purpose is that we be adopted as his children and participate with him in his great destiny for this planet and for all eternity.

Now, if there is high purpose to our lives, in the broadest sense, there must be high purpose to the particular details of our lives as well. This doesn't mean those details are manipulated by some great puppeteer in the sky. It does mean, however, that if we align our lives with God's broader purposes and make our individual decisions within the parameters of those purposes, our lives will unfold with meaning and destiny.

It also means there is a broader picture in which we participate and of which we are a vital part. For people of destiny there is always more going on than meets the eye. We are often involved in divine setups, although it appears to us and everyone else that we are simply going about our usual routines.

One Good Apple

I took a year's break between my second and third year of seminary, when our first daughter was born. I worked at a steel warehouse loading and unloading trucks and train cars full of steel. I often worked with a fellow who had one of the filthiest mouths I've ever heard on a human being. I've been in the army and worked on construction sites where the language turned the air various shades of blue, but Charlie was in a class all his own. He literally could not finish a sentence without vomiting filth everywhere.

For some reason Charlie took a liking to me. He decided he was going to be my friend and curse and swear me right through the day. We'd load trucks together and—oh man! Not only did he swear a lot, he talked a lot. He talked constantly, even when there was nothing to say; then he'd seal it with a curse.

In time I came to like Charlie. He was a unique character,

and he had a great sense of humor. We'd eat lunch together, and he would swear me through lunch. This went on for three or four months. Then one day, as we were eating lunch, he said to me, "Boy, my wife sure likes you."

I didn't know what to make of his comment. Coming from him, it could mean anything. "Charlie, I don't believe I've ever met your wife," I answered.

"No, no, you never have, but she sure likes you."

"Well, you're going to have to help me out here," I said.

"She told me the other day that since I've been working with you, I've been swearing less."

"Really? I hadn't noticed!"

"Yeah, it's true."

"I didn't know you wanted to swear less," I told him. "I thought you talked the way you wanted to."

The man stopped cold and looked at me very soberly. "Jerry, I have tried to stop swearing all my life," he said. "I was raised in a home where I learned swear words before I learned English. I can't remember ever hearing anything else until I started going to school. It's the only way I've ever talked. I'm so embarrassed by the way I talk, I don't go out to dinner or anyplace else, because I know I offend people. But since I've been hanging out with you, I've been talking better, and that's encouraging to me and my wife."

Before I left the job, I had a wonderful chance to pray with Charlie, and we became even better friends. Working with Charlie taught me something about ministry. You see, God has this strange idea. We know that if you have a sack of good apples and you place one rotten apple in the sack, when you come back after a few days, you'll find the bad apple has tainted all the good ones. We know that—but God doesn't. He doesn't understand the principle, and I don't know how it got past him. He honestly believes you can take a sack of rotten apples and put a good apple in the center, come back in a couple of days, and find that the rotten apples have improved because that one good apple is in there. Can you believe it?

Now, you may be the only good apple in the rotten sack of your job or your neighborhood; but God says the place is better because you're there.

I often say at the close of a Sunday sermon, "As we go back into our world tomorrow, don't despise that world. Don't forget that sitting here in this protected environment isn't the real world. Sunday is a good break from the world, but it's not the real world.

> **God says the place is better because you're there.**

We're going back into the world that Jesus redeemed. We're going back not only with the message of redemption, but as those who are in the process of redemption and through whom redemption can take place."

That redemptive process is one of those broader purposes God has for our lives.

While I was working at the warehouse, something was being redeemed in Charlie, and I didn't even realize it. I can't tell you how many times I prayed, "Lord, could you put me with somebody besides Charlie today? I want to work with someone nice." But God put me where he wanted me to be: right next to Charlie.

It was a long time before I could get through the mouth to the person. But when I found him, I found a person Jesus died for—a valuable man.

Because you, too, are in Christ, you can know with absolute certainty that God has put you where he would be if he were you. He has put you there to impact the lives of the people he wants to touch in that place. Knowing you are a recipient of destiny is one of the great benefits of your covenant status.

Adopted into the Family

Barbara and I have an adopted son who came to our family from India as a two-year-old. The fact that Sundar is adopted doesn't mean he's any less mine than my other three children; he's fully mine. And he always will be.

In New Testament times adoption was a very common practice. But in those days an interesting custom was associated with it: the adoptive parents had to agree they would never, ever disinherit their adopted child. A natural-born child could be disinherited but an adopted child couldn't.

There are two ways to become part of a family: you can be born into it, or you can be adopted into it. Do you know that as a believer in Christ, you are in the family of God both ways? Because you are "born again" (see John 3:5–8), you have all the benefits of a natural-born child; you have the legal rights to all the family inheritance and holdings. But according to Ephesians 1:5, you have been adopted into God's family, too, so you also have all the security of an adopted child.

We were willing to wade through all the paperwork and legal procedures to adopt Sundar, because he was chosen. We wanted him. He didn't just show up and give us no choice in the matter; he was desired and planned for. In the same way, you're adopted into God's family and have all the benefits of adoption. God chose you; he saved you from being an orphan.

Here's how Paul puts it: "He predestined us to be adopted as his sons through Jesus Christ, in accordance with his pleasure and will. . . . In him we were also chosen, having been predestined according to the plan of him who works out everything in conformity with the purpose of his will" (Ephesians 1:5, 11).

At one time, although you were alive, you had no place to belong. Now you're in the family of God. What a wonderful covenant blessing!

A Recipient of God's Grace

Another blessing or benefit of God's covenant is expressed in verse 6: "To the praise of his glorious grace, which he has freely given us in the One he loves."

Grace: God's favor, freely given, never earned. When God decided to allow Christ's righteous life to be the substitute for your sinful life, so you could enter into a transforming, life-giving relationship with him—that was grace! If he had decided against the substitution, you would have no court of appeal. You could not obligate him to accept you or force his hand. The terms of the covenant are binding; and because of sin those terms were broken. The just result is alienation from God and all the consequences that alienation entails.

But the wonderful truth is, because you are en Christo, you're not alienated. Instead, you're on a transforming, redeeming journey with God. You're in a life-giving relationship with him! Not because of anything you've done or ever could do; but rather, because God has fulfilled his side of the covenant, and he has allowed Christ to fulfill yours.

That, my friend, is grace. Incredible, isn't it? Surely, if Paul stopped at this point, we would consider ourselves abundantly blessed! But in the next few verses in Ephesians 1, Paul lists five more benefits that come from our covenant relationship with God. We'll look at them in the next chapter.

EMBRACING
Your New
IDENTITY

Have you ever done anything you wished you could wipe out? A decision, a comment, an act you'd like to erase? I'm not a criminal, but there are still things I've done I wish I hadn't and things I've done that people are still recovering from. If only I could go back and undo it all! If that undoing were possible, it would be called *redemption*.

Like most pastors, I meet with lots of people who wish they could undo certain things. Sometimes after a particular meeting, I'll think, *If these folks had planned to mess up their lives, they couldn't have done a better job. They left no stone unturned!* Their situations often appear hopeless. And yet, I've seen Jesus Christ come into many of those "hopeless" situations and redeem them. Where there was chaos and pain, hurt and hopelessness, there is now joy and peace and life.

Redemption

Redemption is one of the covenant benefits we have because we are in Christ. Ephesians 1:7 says, "In him we have redemption through his blood." Because you are in Christ, God promises to take the destruction in your life—even the destruction you've brought on yourself—and cause value to come out of it.

The prophet Isaiah wrote that God gives "the oil of gladness instead of mourning, and a garment of praise instead of a spirit of despair" (Isaiah 61:3). Paul makes one of the Bible's greatest statements about redemption in Romans 8:28: "And we know that in all things God works for the good of those who love him, who have been called according to his purpose."

> God can take that destructive thing and turn it to your benefit—and the benefit of others.

Have you ever caught yourself saying things to yourself that are destructive? "Tell me what you say to yourself on the way to work," I once asked a man in my office. "When you're driving in traffic, what goes through your mind? What are you telling yourself?"

He answered, "I'm telling myself what an idiot I am and what a failure I am, what a bad father I am, what a rotten husband I am. I'm reminding myself of all my stupid words and mistakes."

That's lethal! If you think that way long enough, you will inevitably act out that picture of yourself. That's where redemption steps in. The Scripture says that you are "transformed by the renewing of your mind" (Romans 12:2). The process of redemption helps you think differently. You can stop saying destructive things to yourself. You can take yourself off the sure path toward acting destructively.

"But," you may counter, "you just don't know what I've done."

Thank God I don't ever need to know! But you know and

God knows, and he can redeem whatever it is. He can take that destructive thing and turn it to your benefit—and the benefit of others.

Take Phil, for example. Phil had become hopelessly entangled in pornography and other destructive, sexually addictive behaviors. Then one day his well-constructed secret life crumbled. The ugliness of his addiction was out in the open for all to see, including his horror-stricken wife and family. But the tsunami of destruction had been stopped, and God's redemption, freedom, and healing began the miraculous process of reconstructing a whole new world out of the broken splinters of Phil's life. Today Phil and his wife are the co-directors of an exploding ministry that is bringing that same miracle to other families.

There are so many other examples I could tell you about. One of my friends, who is celebrating twenty-five years of sobriety, is helping dozens of others who struggle with alcohol addiction. He is walking with them as they, through God's grace and strength, walk the road he knows so well. Another friend, almost totally paralyzed by a horrible head-on collision, brings Christ's presence, encouragement, and hope to hundreds of people from her wheelchair.

You know similar stories. Perhaps you *are* one of those stories. Not only does God turn the destruction to your benefit, he uses the scars to benefit and heal others.

Forgiveness of Sins

Ephesians 1:7 tells us, "In him we have redemption through his blood, the forgiveness of sins, in accordance with the riches of God's grace that he lavished on us with all wisdom and understanding."

Part 2: WHO YOU ARE

Guilt is an insidious confidence-stripper. If God wanted us to be completely ineffective persons with no influence anywhere, all he'd have to do is leave us in our guilt. After all, we've all sinned. Guilt is just a part of the package.

Because of Christ's obedience, however, our sins can be forgiven. What does that mean? Well, if you forgive another person, you've chosen not to punish that individual for whatever he or she did to hurt you. That's forgiveness: making the choice not to punish.

Forgiveness does not mean:

- Forgetting. "Forgive and forget"—try pulling that off sometime, and let me know if you succeed!

- Feeling better. There are events so painful in your life that, whenever you remember them, you will always sense the hurt.

- Moving back into a destructive relationship. There are people with whom you may never be able to have a healthy relationship. Some people are so damaged emotionally and socially, they are not capable of sustaining a healthy relationship with anyone. Forgiveness can provide a basis for the reestablishment of a healthy relationship, but it doesn't demand the reinstatement of an unhealthy one.

- Compromising or condoning wrong behavior. Forgiveness doesn't deal with guilt or innocence. Justice deals with guilt and innocence. Your forgiving someone else doesn't mean what that person did was OK. What he or she did may never be OK in anybody's book.

Chapter 5: EMBRACING Your New IDENTITY

Ultimately, forgiveness is not an emotion; it's a *decision*. You don't forgive with your memory or emotions—you forgive with your will. It's a choice you make not to enter into a lifestyle of revenge and punishment, of getting even.

Likewise, when the Bible says God has forgiven you, it means he's not looking to punish you. God is not relating punitively toward you in any way.

The difficulties and problems in your life are not the result of the punishment of God. If that were true, then Ephesians 1:7 couldn't also be true. You can't have it both ways. If you've been forgiven, then you can't still be punished. Biblical forgiveness is relief and release from the threat of punishment. It's a wonderful covenant benefit.

What about Consequences?

"But what about sin?" you may ask. "Shouldn't it have consequences?"

It not only should, it does!

But it doesn't take God to punish sin. When you wake up feeling rotten on the morning after, it's not because God is saying, "You had a bad night, so I'm going to beat you up this morning."

No, it's the stuff you did last night that's making you feel horrible. *Sin punishes sin.* If you sin, you will hurt. Sin hurts. Sin kills. It's the wages of sin that are death; God's gift is eternal life (see Romans 6:23). God is not watching and waiting for you to sin, so he'll have a good reason to take you to the woodshed for a whipping. I've often had Christians tell me, "I guess this bad thing is happening in my life because God is punishing me." I answer, "If that's the case, then what was the cross about? Why did Jesus die?"

Because you're in Christ, there is no punishment from God on you. The Scripture declares that you're saved from the wrath to come. You're not under the curse of the Law. We said this in chapter 1, but it's worth repeating: there is no angry God up there looking to get you.

"Well then, why do all these bad things keep happening to me?"

Let me ask, would they happen to you if you weren't a Christian? Is the fact that you're a believer the reason they're happening? Lots of people who don't believe in God have pretty rough lives. Who's causing their trouble? Are Christians the only ones who suffer, or is God out to get everybody?

I figure, if God is out to punish me, I'm dead. I have no hope, because there is always something he could punish. I'm not a bad person; in fact, I'm better than I used to be. Even so, if he's looking for a reason to punish me, he's got a case. There's no question about it.

But Paul says, "Therefore, there is now no condemnation for those who are in Christ Jesus"—those who choose not to live "according to the sinful nature" (Romans 8:1, 4). We've already established that as a believer you are in Christ. And I think it's safe to assume you've chosen not to live "according to the sinful nature"—that is, at the mercy of your emotions and appetites. Why else would you be reading this book? If you wanted to live a fleshly, sinful life, you would have already lost interest in these pages. You wouldn't have wasted your money buying this book! If you've gotten this far, you must be interested in investigating what it means to follow God.

Well, if there's no condemnation, then there's no basis for punishment. If you are tried in a court of law and acquitted, you don't get sent to jail. It would be preposterous for a judge to announce, "The jury finds you not guilty, so I sentence you to five years in prison." When you're acquitted, there's no condemnation. There's no basis for sentencing. In Christ you're acquitted. You're forgiven.

The Great Opportunist

The problem for most of us is that we don't believe it. Forgiven for what *we've* done? No way! So we punish ourselves in Jesus's name. We even interpret painful circumstances as punishment from God. This is tragic. We live on a planet where bad things happen. Have you noticed? They happen to good people, bad people, and everybody in between. It is a given. It doesn't take God to cause an earthquake on Planet Earth. Disasters on Planet Earth are as predictable as gravity. You'll never jump off a building and go up. You'll always go down.

If you live in this world, it'll hurt. You'll say, "Ouch." At least, I hope you have a theology that lets you say ouch when it hurts. I've met Christians who don't. It hurts but they pretend it doesn't, and they lie to me and tell me it doesn't hurt—all in the name of faith. That's not faith; that's denial.

If it hurts, say, "Ouch!" It's OK. Just know in the midst of the pain, God promises not to leave you without hope, imprisoned on a planet where disasters happen. Instead, he says, "I'm giving you an assignment, so you'll need to stay where you are for a while. It's a dangerous place, I know. But while you're there, in everything that happens, I will be working for your good and my greater purposes."

You see, God is a great opportunist. When disaster strikes, he says, "This has the potential to destroy, but let me step in and work it for your good." Be certain today: if there is pain or chaos and confusion in your life, it's not because God is punishing you. He has forgiven you in Christ! The fact is, you live in a world where tragedies strike, whether you're a follower of God or not. But as a follower of God, you have the awesome privilege of inviting him into that chaos and praying, "Lord, work in this for my good. I can't wait to see what you're going to do."

Forgiveness is based on God's grace, not on our performance. In your personal theology have you made that switch? "I'm OK today, not because I performed well, but because Jesus performed well." Because of him and because we are *in him*, problems and difficulties are just that: problems and difficulties. They are opportunities through which God can work—not evidences of his punishment.

Healthy Obedience

"Since I'm already forgiven," you may ask, "why should I concern myself with obeying God?" Well, let me explain it this way. When I was fourteen years old, I was quite convinced I knew just about everything there was to know. I was also convinced my mother did not, and I was in the process of telling her so, in a very disrespectful voice, when my father happened to enter the room.

My dad was very soft-spoken but physically powerful. Smart

people did not upset him—and few things upset Dad more than someone mistreating his wife. I knew immediately I wasn't smart when he sent me to my room in a tone that assured me negotiation was not an option.

My room was a big area above the garage—a bed in one corner, a Ping-Pong table in the middle, and plenty of space left over. I went up the stairs thinking, *I'm fourteen and a bright guy. What can he do to me?*

Dad came up a little later and sat down on the bed beside me. He was not a happy man. He reached over to take my arm. I moved away. He reached further and I stood up. He stood up, and I took off running around the Ping-Pong table. I was fourteen, smart, and fast. About halfway around the table, though, I realized Dad wasn't following. He was waiting. Even a fourteen-year-old can grasp the futility of running in a closed room when no one is chasing.

> **If there is pain or chaos and confusion in your life, it's not because God is punishing you.**

We sat back down on the bed, and Dad quietly said something that radically changed my relationship with my parents and my view of life.

"Son, I can no longer force you to respect or obey your mom and me. You are coming to the place where you will have to decide to respect and obey us just because you love us."

He stood up, walked out of the room, and shut the door. I stayed glued to my bed, realizing I wasn't as smart as I thought I was.

I wasn't a perfect son from that point on. But my life began to include a principle that only years later I would be able to express:

healthy obedience is based on love, not on performance or fear of punishment.

Jesus said, "If you *love* me, you will obey what I command" (John 14:15). Because of Dad's words that day, I understand Christ's words today.

Obeying God is not a matter of performance. It's not a matter of "being good enough" so he won't punish us. We're forgiven, remember? Rather, obedience is the natural and pure outflowing of love. We love him; therefore, we live in ways that express that love.

A God's-Eye View

Ephesians 1:9 brings up another covenant benefit that is ours in Christ: "And he made known to us the mystery of his will."

As we've said, God is a God of purpose and intention. Reality is intentional. But God's intentions, the "mystery of his will," can only be known by those who are in relationship with him. The good news is, because you are in Christ, you have that relationship! It's a dynamic relationship that not only transforms your life, it radically transforms your perceptions.

That we live in a confused and contradictory world is not a tough case to make. We do away with God in the public square, and we're shocked at godless behavior. We outlaw the teaching of biblical values, and we're stunned when crime increases, justice falters, and children shoot each other at school. We shun covenant marriage and commitment, and we can't figure out why families disintegrate and kids implode. We raise money and pass laws to save endangered bugs at the same time we raise money and pass laws to allow the killing of unborn children, and we wonder why everything in life seems so mixed up.

If there is a way to begin to tap into the "mystery of God's will," now would be an ideal time to do so!

The fact is, we live in a Christ-centered universe—and that which centers the universe must also be the center of our lives, if we want to see things as they really are. Because you are in Christ, your perspective is in the process of transformation. It's becoming the same as his. You're beginning to see things as God sees them, not according to the world's warped view.

The more you center your life on your relationship with God, the more insight you will have into what's really going on in the world. For a believer en Christo, the universe is both personal and purposeful. You have the privilege not only of knowing God's purposes, but of joining him in them, as well.

Included and Marked

Let's look now at the last two benefits of your covenant relationship found in Ephesians 1. Verse 13 says that "you also were included in Christ." Inclusion—what a grand reality! What Paul is expressing here is the radical idea that Jesus Christ was not just a national Messiah, but a universal Savior. Ephesians 2 explains how this process took place. Now, in Jesus, Jews and Gentiles are both reconciled to God, and there is "one new man" (Ephesians 2:15). This releases all the benefits of God's covenant to all who meet in Jesus—including you and me. We'll develop this idea more fully in chapter 8.

You're not only included, however; you're also marked. Ephesians 1:13 continues: "You were marked in him with a seal, the promised Holy Spirit." Let me ask you, is there any evidence of the indwelling of the Holy Spirit in your life? If there is, that evidence is your receipt. It's your proof that you're a child of God. The presence of the Holy Spirit in your life is the deposit guaranteeing your inheritance!

It's so imperative that you understand who you are and what you have in Christ—even on your bad days. Especially on your bad days! You are blessed with every spiritual blessing. You are chosen. You are a recipient of destiny and of God's amazing grace. You have been redeemed from hopelessness and fully forgiven. You have the privilege of knowing God's purposes in the world and joining him in them. You're included in the universal family of God and marked by the Holy Spirit, so your inheritance is assured.

None of these benefits of your covenant relationship with God are dependent on how well you do today or any day. They have to do with how well Jesus did. If, in honest humility, you can allow *his* obedience to be the basis of your relationship with God, then you are en Christo. You are in Christ and he is in you.

Any working of his Holy Spirit in your life reveals the fact that the full inheritance of God is yours. You're a person of the covenant. Because of Christ you have a relationship with God that is transforming your life, your purpose, and your potential. You have truly experienced a new birth.

Until you understand this—until you recognize who you are in Christ and begin to appropriate all the covenant benefits that are yours en Christo—your confidence, courage, and trust in God will be spasmodic and unpredictable at best. But once you embrace your new identity in all its fullness, you will have confidence, courage, and trust to a degree you've never known. You will be fully equipped and ready to be the church on Monday.

YOU ARE
What You
BELIEVE

Many believers are committed to Christ but not equipped with a Christian philosophy. Quite often we don't *think* Christianly. Consequently, we still see the world through a warped and clouded lens. A fallen culture has given us a distorted perspective, a worldview overlaid by cultural tints and filters that block us from true understanding. Though Christian, we view life in a very secular way.

That is why every Christian needs a workable, practical philosophy of life. As we learned in the last chapter, one of the covenant benefits of being in Christ is insight into "the mystery of his will" (Ephesians 1:9). That's a wonderful blessing! But as we grow in our relationship with God, we also need to be developing our personal theology—a biblical belief system that is coherent and makes sense. A truly scriptural theology will help build the confidence and courage we need to be the church on Monday.

A Timely Prayer

Paul's prayer in Ephesians 1:15–19 is keenly appropriate for us in that regard. It unlocks the keys to breaking away from a distorted worldview and thinking Christianly instead:

> For this reason, ever since I heard about your faith in the Lord Jesus and your love for all the saints, I have not stopped giving thanks for you, remembering you in my prayers. I keep asking that the God of our Lord Jesus Christ, the glorious Father, may give you the Spirit of wisdom and revelation, so that you may know him better. I pray also that the eyes of your heart may be enlightened in order that you may know the hope to which he has called you, the riches of his glorious inheritance in the saints, and his incomparably great power for us who believe.

The apostles prayed many prayers that were not recorded in Scripture. But some prayers were so significant, so uniquely inspired by the Holy Spirit, they were made a part of the revelation of God for the church in all ages. This is one of those prayers. It is more than a local prayer for a church in the distant past. This is a prayer intended for us too.

Let me suggest a wonderful personal study: Go through the Gospels and the Epistles, and read each of the recorded prayers—those prayed by Jesus and those prayed by the apostles. Ask, "Why is this recorded? What is important about this prayer?" Allow the Holy Spirit to share with you why each one is included in the Scriptures.

Chapter 6: YOU ARE What You BELIEVE

Knowing God

Many people have misconceptions about prayer. Prayer does not persuade a reluctant God to act. God is not sitting in a big recliner in the sky, waiting for us to say the right words so he can get up and move. Who would be God if he needed our prayers in order to take action? *We* would be God!

God isn't in a recliner; he's on a throne. But our personal theology often puts God in the wrong chair. It places us in the precarious position of telling God what to do, when to do it, and how to get it done. The next time you look in the mirror, remind yourself: you're looking at someone made in the image of God, but you're not looking at God!

Prayer, whatever else it may be, is the means by which you and I get insight into what God is doing in our world, the action he is taking at the present time. We enter into his plan through prayer. We receive his perspective through prayer.

With these thoughts in mind, let's look at the details of Paul's prayer in Ephesians 1:15. Remember, he's praying for you and me! He begins, "For this reason, ever since I heard about your faith in the Lord Jesus and your love for all the saints . . ." Those are two of the fundamental qualities of Christian people: faith in the Lord Jesus and love for all the saints.

That's *all* the saints.

"But what if they're the wrong denomination? What if I disagree with their doctrine?"

Amazingly, Paul just throws us all together, disregarding our differences. That bothers me, because I think doctrine is important, and I expect other Christians to be spiritual in the same way I am, don't you? But Paul's wording is no mistake. I'd say that for a man born over two thousand years ago, he knows us pretty well.

His prayer then follows with two requests. The first is that "God . . . may give you the Spirit of wisdom and revelation." Notice the word *Spirit* is capitalized, indicating that it refers to the Holy Spirit. In other words, Paul is asking God to give us the Holy Spirit in a way and to a degree that makes wisdom and revelation ours. The

> **"Who is God?"
> is not a
> multiple-choice
> question.**

second request is that "the eyes of your heart may be enlightened." We might say it this way: "that the lights of your heart be turned on."

Why does Paul make these requests? Verse 17 tells us: so we may know God better.

Our knowing of God, you see, has to transcend human logic, learning, and understanding. I don't know about you, but I have a tendency to become cerebral in my Christianity and in my life in general. I enjoy the study of philosophy; I have enjoyed it ever since my university days. I like everything to be neat, concise, and logical. There's nothing wrong with that—unless I limit my approach to God to that which seems neat, concise, and logical to me. It would be a mistake to demand that reality agree with my sometimes flawed logic and warped perception of God.

I was recently talking with someone about the trouble many people have with God—including many Christians—because of all the suffering and pain they see in the world. They ask, "What kind of a God would permit accidents and pain?" "How can you love a God who allows these things?" "If God is good, how can so many bad things happen?" That's a cerebral approach. The questions are valid; but to a certain degree, the answers transcend our mental capabilities and logic.

The God of Popular Culture

The God revealed by the Holy Spirit is very different from the God of popular culture. Many Christians today are trying to embrace and love a cultural God who is not like the God revealed in Jesus Christ.

Our cultural God, for example, is responsible for the bad things that take place in the world and not so much for the good things. When something catastrophic happens, it's an "act of God." Even our insurance policies refer to certain disasters that way. But when something good happens, we're more likely to credit "luck" than God. Think about it. If there is an accident and people are killed, we ask, "Why did God allow that?" If, on the other hand, the same terrible accident takes place and nobody is hurt, we say, "Boy, were they lucky!" The cultural message is, "You're better off with luck than you are with God." From there it's an easy step to, "Why bother with God?"

But "Who is God?" is not a multiple-choice question. Popular culture doesn't get to decide. There is only one God, and he's the one Jesus revealed. Moreover, Jesus revealed him fully. It's not that Jesus showed us only the good side of God. There is no other side. The God Jesus revealed—the only God there is—is not a good God on some days and a capricious tormentor on others.

In order to be truly Christian, you must have a theology that centers on a predictably good God. A God who never, in any way, involves himself with evil. A God who is good in the way you understand good, not good in the way someone redefines it. If God is even slightly or remotely connected to evil, we are all in deep trouble.

"OK—then why the mess?" you may ask. "If God is so good, why is the world so bad? Why doesn't he step up and do something? Who is this God anyway?"

This is precisely the point of Paul's prayer: that we might know God. Really know him—not just know about him, or about the cultural perceptions of him. Paul wants us to know God as he truly is. He wants us to understand what he's really like.

Did you ever experience something painful or tragic? Why? Why did God let it happen? Did he stop loving you? Did you do something wrong and make him mad that day? Is he really, after all, trying to punish you for your sin? Maybe you didn't read your Bible enough that morning. But then, how much is enough? If only you would have known sooner, you could have added another chapter!

If this is the way you think about God, face it: you'll never know soon enough.

My son and I were having a conversation after he realized he'd done a rather stupid thing, as young people sometimes do. "I guess I just learn things the hard way," he said.

"You can learn a lesson the hard way," I replied, "but it's usually a bit late. By the time you've learned it the hard way, you're already wiping the blood off your face. It would be less painful to learn it earlier."

Chapter 6: YOU ARE What You BELIEVE

Ever heard the old adage, "Experience is a cruel teacher, but fools will learn from none other"?

Is God to Blame for Evil?

Let's come at this issue of pain, suffering, and evil from a different direction. Let's suppose the evil in the world is not God's fault at all. Suppose it got here totally aside from his action. And here's a thought even more disturbing: suppose the ones who are really responsible for all this pain, suffering, and evil are the people we see in the mirror every day. Maybe it's our fault; maybe we're the ones causing the problems.

An uncomfortable thought, yes, but it's an important possibility for us to consider. The fact is, when God created the world and gave it to us, there were no disasters. There was no evil, no pain. There weren't even weeds or thistles! And we had an opportunity to continue living in that pristine condition, because God gave the world to us as a present. It wasn't a conditional offering. God didn't say, "If you treat the earth well, you'll keep it. If you don't, I'll take it back."

We received the gift and accepted dominion over it. That meant whatever we chose to do with it, from that point on, would have a universal impact. Our decisions would dictate conditions on the planet. God gave that power to us.

Let's suppose that at the beginning this arrangement worked perfectly well. But then, at a crucial moment, we gave our dominance away to someone else: Satan, the personification of evil. It was, after all, ours to give. When we gave away our power, evil had entrance to work. Sickness and death, violence and disasters entered the world—not because of some twisted plan of God, but because *we* chose to give to Satan what God had given to us.

Let's take this line of thinking a bit further. Suppose that even though God gave us unconditional dominion, when he saw what we did with it, he didn't walk away in disgust. He didn't give up on mankind. Instead, he acted in a way that would preserve our freedom of choice and, at the same time, provide an opportunity for our choice to be reconsidered.

Suppose he decided to act into the chaos we had created—to intervene in a way that could be redemptive for us. Suppose he decided to provide a way for us to once again relate to him, so we could get a second chance and find hope for the future.

It would be a remarkable thing, wouldn't it?

If this theory happened to be part of your personal theology, it would take God off the hook for causing evil—which, if you were ever in trouble, would be very important. If the person you need to go to for help is the same person who is causing the problem, you have a distinct dilemma on your hands, right? If the police chief is known to be the thief who is stealing from you, what hope do you have that calling the police department will bring you protection from burglary? If God is the one causing the pain in your life, it seems rather ridiculous to think you would go to him for help and healing. If he is part of the problem, he is blocked from being any part of the solution.

A Predictably Good God

Do you see the dilemma you've got if you don't have a predictably good God? I don't know how you're going to work it out theologically, but somehow you've got to emerge from your theological tunnel with a God who is predictably good every minute of every day. Whenever evil happens to you, you need to be able to declare, with utter confidence and complete understanding of who God is, "God is not causing this, and God has not allowed it. Instead, he has acted into this pain with his own life."

Indeed, God declares through the cross: "No, I won't allow this. I will bring a resolution to the pain in your life. You can come to me with confidence, because I am an ever-present help in time of need." When you're sick, you can ask God for healing; he's not the one making you sick. When you're struggling, you can ask God for relief; he's not the one causing your trouble.

If you don't have a predictably good God, you've got foolishness for faith. If you're going to bother to have a God at all, then you need a predictably good God, or you're in chaos.

Satan's Timeworn Lie

The lie that Satan has woven into every civilization since Adam is that God has a hidden mean streak. "Has God told you this?" Satan asked Eve. When she answered in the affirmative, he insinuated that God had an ulterior motive: "Well, yes, but he knows something else; he's hiding something. There's a divine mean streak at work here, and he can't be fully trusted." That's Satan's historic, original lie, and it's still prevalent in our belief systems today.

When Paul prays, "May the Spirit of wisdom and revelation allow you to know him, to understand him," he's asking for the Holy Spirit to work in us, so our cultural misunderstandings about God are exposed for what they are, and we come to know who God really is: someone with whom we are totally and utterly safe.

Part 2: WHO YOU ARE

My heavenly Father is at least as good a parent as I am. If you are a parent, these illustrations are easy to comprehend: Do you try to think up painful things to do to your children, just so they can learn a lesson? Do you teach them not to cross the street in traffic by pushing them in front of a car when it goes by? Do you teach them to be careful going down stairs by pushing them down a stairway? Do you teach your children by setting up disasters for them?

I hope not! In our society the law requires those in certain professions to report parents who do such things. Their children can be taken away from them. If I were doing that, my children might, by some strange twist, love me, but they would never be foolish enough to trust me.

That's precisely what many Christians do: they love God, but they don't trust him.

In this world it doesn't take an act of God for bad things to happen. Bad things happen because of our actions—the accumulation of our rebellion. Our choices were determinative for the whole planet; and when our actions, in Adam, became rebellious, rebellion dominated the planet. Everything, including nature itself, was twisted out of place. Everything is out of order.

But God has acted into this hopeless chaos. The Scripture says, "In all things God works for the good of those who love him" (Romans 8:28). This is true even in your deepest pain, your greatest struggle, your worst nightmare.

God Is for Us

Two weeks ago a mother came to my office in deep pain. Caitlin had been a professional athlete before she was married in her thirties. Sadly, their first child died through disease. Their second child was born dead. She then endured two miscarriages before finally giving birth to a healthy little boy. Now Caitlin was pregnant again—and she was terrified. I could understand why!

As we talked she shared some serious questions she had about the deaths of her other children. I was so thankful that I could say to her, "Caitlin, God had no part in the taking of the lives of those children. He doesn't murder little babies. What he has done is act into your life in such a way that you will forfeit no time with them at all. He has acted in a way that reserves them in heaven for you. They're yours; you will hold them in heaven. You miss them now, but there's hope; they are not lost eternally.

> God works for the good—even in your deepest pain, your greatest struggle, your worst nightmare.

"I'll even take it a step further," I told her. "I believe they will recognize you, and you will recognize them. You will miss nothing of mothering those lost children."

God is good! How wonderful to know you can look into the face of your deepest pain and say, "Thank you, Lord, because you are not the one causing this; you did not set this up to teach me a lesson. Instead, you will step into this struggle with me and cause it to work for my good, somehow, some way. You will even make me better for it."

There are times when God does step in and miraculously heal. He reserves that right. Have you, or has someone you know, been physically healed by the power of the Holy Spirit? Why does he do that? First of all, he heals because he really doesn't want you to hurt. Second, every time you hear of someone being healed, God is reassuring you, "I'm on the side of health and healing and life." Miraculous healing doesn't happen all the time, but it happens consistently enough to be an illustration of which side God is on. We have a God who is for us and not against us.

It can be difficult to come to grips with the fact that God is predictably good. But if your personal belief system leads you to anything less than a predictably good God, *you don't have a Christian theology.*

I can't work out all the wrinkles for you, but you're going to have to come to a belief in a good God, or why have a God at all? We can't trust a God with a mean streak. No wonder we need the Spirit of wisdom and revelation! It's only in coming to know who God really is that we discover a God who is predictably good. We can love him. We can trust him. We can appropriate all his covenant blessings with confidence.

In the final analysis we are what we believe. When we believe in a God who is predictably good, we are truly Christian.

We are the church on Monday.

Part 3

WHAT YOU HAVE

HOPE, WEALTH, and POWER

In the last chapter we began looking at Paul's prayer in Ephesians 1:15–19. As we noted, this is not simply a prayer for a group of Christians in the city of Ephesus in the first century; the Holy Spirit made sure it was recorded in the canon of Scripture because it has implications for Christians everywhere and at all times. It still has great relevance for you and me today.

I want us to look more closely now at the last two verses: "I pray also that the eyes of your heart may be enlightened in order that you may know the hope to which he has called you, the riches of his glorious inheritance in the saints, and his incomparably great power for us who believe."

In this passage Paul asks for the lights to come on in your heart so that you will know three things:

1. "The *hope* to which he has called you"

2. "The *riches* of his glorious inheritance"

3. "His incomparably great *power* for us who believe"

I like to pray this prayer for myself, because I am well aware of the dullness that can creep into my heart over time. In my work I spend the majority of my time with really nice Christian people. But most believers do not. Most Christians work in the midst of a fallen culture, a fallen world. I understand that. I've been there.

Here's the danger: the influence of the culture we live in brings dimness to our hearts and shadows to our spiritual perceptions. I work mostly with Christians, but I'm still impacted by the cultural messages I see and hear every day. The silt and sludge and smog of fallenness begins to collect on our hearts and minds until we forget the things we once knew and fail to understand the things we do remember. That's why I pray, "O Christ Jesus, enlighten the eyes of my heart! Keep the lights of my heart turned on."

When our hearts begin to get dark, we lose focus on the three things that are key to knowing who we are and what we have in Christ: our hope, our inheritance, and our power. Let's look at each of these keys individually.

An Amazing Hope

Our hope as Christians is based on the knowledge that we are not limited by the world's systems or solutions. Because we are in Christ, we have hope beyond what can take place politically, economically, and sociologically in our world. We are not dependent on political or social structures for our future; we have resources that transcend the world's meager supply.

You see, we may live in a particular country, but we are citizens of another kingdom. It's not that we're off in the clouds somewhere; it's that our citizenship is based on the presence of God in our lives and in our world, not on our nationality or place of birth.

Chapter 7: HOPE, WEALTH, and POWER

The Antidote to Fear

Since we are not locked into the systems of this world, we can, as Christians, act redemptively into those systems. When our hearts become dull, however, we forget that we have this capacity, and fear sets in. We observe the trends, the politics, the sociology, and we begin to think, "Maybe there's no hope."

> **Our citizenship is based on the presence of God in our lives.**

I love living in Seattle; it's a wonderful city. But our news headlines regularly record senseless acts of violence. How easy it would be to be afraid! Thankfully, as a Christian, I know there's more going on in the world than what I read on the front page.

As believers we can have courage, not because we're stupid, but because we have hope. How do you threaten people who can't die? I've been with Christians who have faced the threat of death. They had to understand where their hope was. It was not in personal heroism; it was not a matter of being tough. Because they were in Christ, they knew they had hope beyond the threat of death.

While speaking in Europe, I was asked to go to Croatia, invited by a group that had translated my book *Love, Acceptance, and Forgiveness* into Croatian. These people had formed a strong church in the city of Pula, which is right across the Adriatic Sea from the boot of Italy, on a point of land reaching into the sea. Our host was a young man who had been a gang leader on the streets of Pula. He gave his life to Christ and is now pastoring a congregation made up of both Croatian and Serbian people.

In the center of Pula stands an almost completely intact Roman coliseum. It was an impressive sight as we drove from the airport to our hotel. I was delighted when I was taken to see the great structure up close and allowed to experience a bit of its history.

Pula, you see, was a favorite vacation spot for the Roman emperors, including Trajan and Nero. Christians were martyred in that very coliseum. While I was there, I crossed the grass arena to the grate covering the lions' entrance. I can't begin to describe the emotions that flooded me as I remembered the saints who were forced to stand in the arena, naked and greased with animal fat, so the lions would spring from their doorway, attack the Christians, and tear them to pieces.

Spectators gambled on how much time it would take the lions to kill the last Christian. It was sport, like wagering at a horse race. I'm sure the Christians were terrified, as any of us would be; but history records that many martyrs, instead of screaming, joined hands and sang or knelt and praised the Lord. These courageous men and women knew the hope to which Christ had called them.

I stood there and wept as I realized what my faith cost. People died for what I believe and hold dear. Christianity is not a fad! Down through the centuries I could almost hear their praying, their singing.

At that time, nineteen centuries ago, most observers would have assumed the Christians were the losers and cruelty was the winner. But the Pula coliseum, the former torture chamber of Christian martyrs, is now the site of Christian praise gatherings, where thousands stand with upraised hands, proclaiming Jesus as Lord. Who is the winner now?

Chapter 7: HOPE, WEALTH, and POWER

Death Is Not a Loss

One of the things Jesus did when he came to earth was to destroy death. The way you are today is as dead as you're going to get. How do I know that? Because the Scripture teaches that when you go through the process we call death, there's nothing lost; there are only things added. Mortality puts on immortality (see 1 Corinthians 15:50–56). I would say that's a plus rather than a minus, wouldn't you?

The Scripture asks two incredible questions of death: "Where is your victory?" and "Where is your sting?" In other words, "Where is your power to hurt us?" These questions are preceded by a remarkable statement: "Death has been swallowed up in victory" (1 Corinthians 15:54). Isn't that amazing? How do you threaten someone who knows death has been defeated? Because we are in Christ, we have hope. We can act courageously into the rottenness of this world, and we don't have to fear its pollution. The worst this world can do to us is hand us our victory.

A Glorious Inheritance

Too often, when the culture around us begins to dull our hearts, we lose focus on the amazing resources available to us. It's so important that we know what is ours in Christ! That's why Paul prays for us to know not only "the hope to which he has called you," but also "the riches of his glorious inheritance in the saints." To put it simply: Know the family fortune! Know the kind of family you're in and the resources that it owns—the resources that are at your disposal.

I know when my own heart gets dull, I begin to forget who I am. I have to remind myself: My heavenly Father really is *somebody*. I may appear destitute, but I'm not at all. Psalm 24:1 declares, "The earth is the LORD's, and everything in it, the world, and all who live in it." Abundant resources are available to me because I'm in the family of God.

Whenever we lose focus and begin to think and plan like the fallen culture does, we need the Holy Spirit to turn the lights on in our hearts and challenge us, "Where is your trust level? What are you trusting in?" We need to remember the riches that are part of our glorious inheritance in Christ. We have resources we don't even know about yet! And we have a heavenly Father who promises to supply all our needs "according to his glorious riches" (Philippians 4:19).

Incomparably Great Power

The third thing Paul prays for us to know in Ephesians 1:19 is God's "incomparably great power for us who believe." He goes on to describe that power in verses 19–23:

> That power is like the working of his mighty strength, which he exerted in Christ when he raised him from the dead and seated him at his right hand in the heavenly realms, far above all rule and authority, power and dominion, and every title that can be given, not only in the present age but also in the one to come. And God placed all things under his feet and appointed him to be head over everything for the church, which is his body, the fullness of him who fills everything in every way.

How much power does it take to raise a dead man? I could stage an impressive display in front of a tomb but never raise a dead man to life. I could place a powerful bomb at the opening, blow a crater in the ground, and the dead man would simply be blown apart. He would not come out of the tomb. The issue, you see, is not simply how much power; it's also what kind of power.

Ephesians 1:19–20 announces that the power at work in you and me is exactly the same power that raised Jesus from the dead. Isn't that phenomenal? It's more than a big bang. There is something working in us that death cannot overcome, that evil can't manipulate.

Defining Evil

What is evil spelled backward? L-I-V-E. Evil is simply that which works against life. So when I say to you that this amazing power is working *life* in you, I mean it's neutralizing the *evil* that is part of your inner world. It is taking evil and turning it inside out. The power that's working in you is the power that raised Jesus from the dead. If death can't overcome it, what can any lesser evil do?

This power not only raised Jesus, it gave him a completely new means of expression—a new body. Think about it: Jesus didn't come out of the tomb crippled. He arose scarred, but not crippled. And the scars were for our sake, not his. Jesus didn't limp out asking for directions to the local hospital, alive, but just barely. He arose! That was it. He arose. And the power that made that possible is now working in you.

I don't know what this incredible fact does for you, but I know what it does for me. I have times when discouragement takes over and hopelessness sets in. When I look at my world with a dull heart, I don't see any way out. But then I remember the "incomparably great power" that's at work in me through Christ. And suddenly, I have hope. I have resources. And I have all the power I need to make it through.

I often talk with people who don't have the energy to even hope again. They feel powerless; their circumstances seem utterly beyond remedy. What can I say? "I pray the Holy Spirit will enlighten the eyes of your heart." When the lights come on, then they will see the incomparably great power that's working in them.

Never forget: even in your weakest moment, the power working in you is the very same power that raised Jesus Christ from the dead. You always have reason for great hope. Your family inheritance is adequate to meet any demand.

Sign Your Name

As we said, when Paul prayed this prayer in Ephesians 1 two thousand years ago, he reached down through the ages, and through the inspiration of the Holy Spirit, he prayed it for *you*. You can write yourself right into this prayer. You can accept its assurance for yourself. You can sign your name to it.

I have a friend who reads through the Bible often. When he finds a particular verse he likes, he writes his initials in the margin. He's now an old man, and his Bible is scribbled all over. It's a mess.

"Why do you do that?" I asked.

"It's just my way of declaring, That's for me; that's my promise," he said.

Ephesians 1:15–23 is for you. It's your promise—every word of it. It's God's intention for you as a believer in Christ.

So go ahead. Put your initials in the margin. Then, whenever you sense your heart is getting dull, go back to the page and pray, "Turn the light on, Holy Spirit."

And he will.

He will.

Chapter 8

ALIVE
and
FREE

It may not be a happy memory, but sometimes it's good to sit down and remember what you used to be like. Isn't God doing a good job? Aren't you turning out better than you thought you would? If you are in Christ, your answer should be a resounding yes!

Ephesians 2 begins with this description of your life before Christ: "As for you, you were dead in your transgressions and sins, in which you used to live when you followed the ways of this world and of the ruler of the kingdom of the air." Before you were in Christ, you were spiritually dead. You were completely cut off from your life-support system, which is a relationship with God. We talked about this in chapter 1. When mankind was created, we were not only biologically alive; we were also spiritually alive through an intimate relationship with God. When that intimate relationship was severed by sin, we began a death spiral.

But you were more than dead; you were victimized. You thought you were in charge of your own life, ordering your own steps. But that wasn't the reality at all. You were being led around, not merely by "the ways of the world" and your own faulty ideas, but by a manipulative ruler. A personification of evil was meddling in your life. Verse 2 identifies him as "the ruler of the kingdom of the air." Then it zeroes in even more: "the spirit who is now at work in those who are disobedient."

So you were spiritually dead, *and* you were a victim. Disobedience is not only an action; it's the result of the influence of a spirit.

I remember a conversation I had with my youngest daughter when she was about eleven. We were living in Oregon in a wonderful house for raising kids—nothing fancy, just a big old home with a heated swimming pool in the backyard. I was studying by the pool one day when Christi came out to sit beside me. As we dangled our feet in the water, she asked a question.

> Disobedience is not only an action; it's the result of the influence of a spirit.

"Daddy, you know, sometimes when you tell me to do something, I don't want to do it. Maybe I wanted to do it until you told me to, and then after you told me, I didn't want to do it anymore. Why is that?"

Whose kid is this wonderful person? I thought to myself. Then I answered, "Honey, two things are going on. The first is that you're becoming your own person. You're becoming a young woman and beginning to have ideas and thoughts of your own. That's a very important process. You're becoming a person who has her own beliefs, one who doesn't just follow everybody else around. That's part of what's going on.

"But there's something else going on too. It's called rebellion. You see, there's a fine line between becoming independent, which is good, and being deliberately disobedient, which is rebellion."

"Oh, I don't want to be rebellious," she quickly assured me.

And do you know, remarkably, that little girl never was. She never, ever went through a rebellious phase in her development. There were times when she needed a reminder: "This is the way we do it in this house." But there was never a reactive smirk or bad attitude.

Not long ago Christi and I were fishing, and I asked her if she remembered that conversation. She did. "I just made a decision that day that I didn't want to be rebellious," she explained.

"I'm so grateful you did," I told her. "I wish every kid would make that decision."

What Christi decided, at the tender age of eleven, was not to be influenced by the spirit of disobedience. At many key points over the years, that spirit would make a play for her attitude, life, and direction. What a different life she would have had if she had not made that choice early in her adolescence!

The Results of Alienation

Ephesians 2:3 continues: "All of us also lived among them at one time, gratifying the cravings of our sinful nature and following its desires and thoughts. Like the rest, we were by nature objects of wrath." What a terrible picture of an alienated person! Before Christ you were dead in your trespasses and sins, victimized by the spirit of disobedience, *and* driven by your appetites and emotions.

If It Feels Good . . .

Driven by appetites and emotions: that's not only a clear description of your life without God; it's also a description of our current culture. How many products are sold to us by appealing to our appetites and emotions? A TV commercial tells us to buy a certain car because "it feels good"—and we do it! It's as if our emotions and appetites are commands to act. If we question those commands, our culture tells us, we are somehow being untrue to ourselves.

Nothing could be further from the truth. We don't have to act in response to our emotions. As Christians we are called to act not on the basis of our emotions, but on the basis of our new values in Christ. In most instances how you feel should have absolutely no bearing on whether you take action or not. In fact, if you see your emotions as a command to act, I'd say you are a very dangerous person!

Think about it: Your feelings will change between the time you get out of bed and the time you brush your teeth. You will experience several mood changes before lunch. How can you make something as nebulous and transitory as your emotions the directing force of your life?

You may explain a certain action by saying, "I couldn't help it. I just felt like it." Well, you may have just felt like it, but you certainly *could* have helped it. You do make choices!

Your will and your emotions are two different parts of you. Your will makes the decisions. The question is, based on what? Emotions are a poor basis, because they're simply reflections of your perception of reality. They don't tell you what's true. They tell you what you *perceive* to be true. That's all. When your perception of reality changes, what will your emotions do? They'll change.

I remember walking home from school one day as a third or fourth grader, when I suddenly sensed that someone was following me. I had heard stories about children being kidnapped, so my adrenaline instantly began pumping. Fearfully, I turned and looked back just in time to see a figure dart behind a tree. Now I began running. I heard the person's footsteps chasing after me. I was too terrified to turn around and look again.

I ran all the way home and up the steps of my front porch. The kidnapper—the murderer—leaped up onto the porch behind me. Then, before I could get inside, he grabbed me.

The next thing I knew, he was laughing. I recognized the voice and turned around. It was Joe, my friend from across the street, playing a joke on me.

It had always been Joe. There never had been a kidnapper. But my perception of reality was that I was being chased by a kidnapper, so what did my emotions do? They responded appropriately to that perception—they added speed to my feet and pounding to my heart. When my perception changed, what happened? The adrenaline fueling my flight exploded in laughter, and Joe and I collapsed on the porch, rolling and holding our sides.

"You were afraid, weren't you?" Joe teased.

"No, of course not! I knew it was you all the time."

Destroyed by Perception

That's why we must choose to act on the basis of our values, not on the basis of our emotions. Emotions reveal perception, not truth. For example, when your emotions announce, "I'm no longer in love with my spouse; I just don't feel like loving this person anymore," you need to remember those feelings only reveal your perception of things at the time. The reality is, you choose to love; and when you got married, you chose to love for life. Yet sadly, too many marriages break up and too many families are destroyed because of emotions based on inaccurate perceptions.

Not long ago I was with a young husband and wife who were going through this very struggle. After the wife described all their problems, I asked, "*Why* are you still together? You don't have to be. You certainly have the money to get a divorce or move out. Why haven't you done that?"

She thought for a bit. "I guess I just don't know."

"OK," I responded, "that's what you need to find out. You need to find out not what your problems are, but why you're still together. There's a reason why you're in here talking to me about this. Those are the reasons we must look for. We need to get beyond the emotions of the moment and find out why you both are still here."

"Well, it must be the children," she ventured.

"That's a good reason."

A selfish culture assumes "the children" are not a good enough reason for a couple to stay together. Excuse me! I think children are valuable enough for two people to make a decision to stick together, work out their problems, and raise their kids. Parents need to ask God to soften their hearts and help them get their act together. Most children would certainly vote for that!

> **You are a victim no longer.**

Sure, there are some relationships that are hopelessly destructive. When hearts are hard, God himself can't change the marriage. But when two people allow the Holy Spirit to soften their hearts, take them past their emotions, change their perceptions of reality, and see one another as Jesus sees them, there is hope.

If you continually use your emotions as reasons to act, you may very well lose some of the most precious things in your life! Thankfully, you don't have to. These verses in Ephesians 2:1–3 describe your *former* life. You're in Christ now. Living at the mercy of your emotions and appetites is *not* part of your new life in him. You are a victim no longer. Instead, you are a person of self-mastery, a person who can make smart choices to live honorably and do the right things.

How is this possible? The answer begins with God's own nature.

The Character of God

Ephesians 2:4–5 says, "But because of his great love for us, God, who is rich in mercy, made us alive with Christ even when we were dead in transgressions—it is by grace you have been saved." And God not only made us alive:

> God raised us up with Christ and seated us with him in the heavenly realms in Christ Jesus, in order that in the coming ages he might show the incomparable riches of his grace, expressed in his kindness to us in Christ Jesus. For it is by grace you have been saved, through faith—and this not from yourselves, it is the gift of God—not by works, so that no one can boast. For we are God's workmanship, created in Christ Jesus to do good works, which God prepared in advance for us to do. (vv. 6–10)

Part 3: WHAT YOU HAVE

This passage lists four great characteristics of God:

- He is loving.

- He is merciful.

- He is gracious.

- He is kind.

The Scriptures declare these attributes of God will never change (see Malachi 3:6 and Hebrews 13:8). If he was ever loving, he is eternally loving. If he was ever merciful, he is eternally merciful. These are his qualities to the absolute. We have a God who is loving, merciful, gracious, and kind—forever and ever.

These character traits are the reason that trusting God is a rational choice. When we believe God and accept his Son as our Savior, we're not making a senseless leap into blind faith and hoping it will work out. Instead, we're making a considered choice to place our trust in someone who will never betray it; someone who has proven himself completely trustworthy.

Because of God's unchanging character, you can trust that you have, indeed, been saved by grace. You can trust that being in Christ makes you a new creation.

"Dead, victimized, and driven" can never again appear on your life's résumé. Those three words have been replaced by new ones: alive, free, raised up, saved, en Christo. You are God's workmanship, created in Christ Jesus to do good works, which God prepared in advance for you to do.

You are the church on Monday.

TRANSFORMED
and
COURAGEOUS

A radical transformation takes place when you enter into a relationship with God through Christ. The transformation is so massive and so total that Jesus called it a "new birth." Four things stand out about you in this transition from old to new, dead to alive. You have:

- A new power source
- A new position
- A new potential
- A new purpose

In the last chapter I suggested that it's good to remember what you used to be like before Christ. One caution, though: just because you still remember and perhaps even struggle with some of the "junk" from your former life, don't minimize the dramatic changes God is producing in you. It's easy to suppose God is merely tweaking some old patterns—making minor adjustments—and think to yourself, *Well, at least I'm getting better.*

A more accurate view is that you are a totally brand-new person! Yes, you have a memory of your former self. Certain habits and attitudes may still reflect the old person. But that's not who you are anymore. You're not just a bad person getting better. You are a new creature in Christ Jesus, and the old things *are* passing away (see 2 Corinthians 5:17). They're on their way out, not because you are working on them, but because there's a new life principle working in you.

Because you're new, the old can't last. The newness is replacing all that is obsolete. A new person is emerging, not because the old one is changing a little bit at a time, but because you *are* a new person. You are complete in Christ. Colossians 2:10 says, "You have been given fullness in Christ." You're fully who he wants you to be. And you're in the process of becoming who you really are.

The list of the fruit of the Spirit in Galatians 5:22–23 creates a snapshot of you as a redeemed child of God. If you want a picture of what you look like to God, there it is. You are a loving, joyful, peaceful, patient, kind, good, faithful, gentle, and self-controlled person.

"Excuse me, I don't think so," you may object. "Obviously, you don't know me very well."

No, the truth is, *you* don't know yourself very well. To live any other way is to live *below* your true identity. What God does is establish your identity and then pull you up into it. You're in that process—being pulled up! God deals with you according to your true identity: a new creation in Christ with a new power source, a new position, a new potential, and a new purpose.

Chapter 9: TRANSFORMED and COURAGEOUS

A New Power Source

Ephesians 2:4–5 says, "Because of his great love for us, God, who is rich in mercy, made us alive with Christ even when we were dead." You have a new life source. The plug is back in the wall! That's what Jesus did; you were disconnected from your life-support system, but he put the plug back in. You now have a direct, intimate relationship with God in which the kiss of God, the breath of God, gives new life to your spirit.

Do you remember when Jesus came into the room where his disciples had gathered after the resurrection? John 20:22 says that "he breathed on them and said, 'Receive the Holy Spirit.'" That's the same phraseology used in Genesis 2:7: "The LORD God formed the man from the dust of the ground and *breathed into his nostrils the breath of life*, and the man became a living being." In Genesis life was given to the first Adam. In Jesus, the second Adam, life has been given to a new race of people—those who are in Christ.

A New Position

Because you have been given new life in Christ, you also have a new position. You live in a different place now, a new neighborhood.

"Well, I still have the same house and the same mortgage payments."

That's true. But Ephesians 2:6 continues, "God raised us up with Christ and seated us with him in the heavenly realms in Christ Jesus." According to this verse, you have a new position—an "in Christ" position, seated in "the heavenly realms."

Understand, by "heavenly realms" we're not talking about a geographic location; so don't try too hard to figure out how you can be here on earth and up there somewhere too. No, your new position has to do with being in the presence of God. It's tied to the truth that because you are in Christ, Christ dwells in you. You are consistently, constantly, and moment-by-moment in his presence. And to live in his presence is to live in heavenly places in Christ Jesus.

It does no good to be in his presence, however, if you're not *aware* of being in his presence. If you have Christ living in you but you are unaware that he's there, you will live as though he's not. That doesn't necessarily mean you will live sinfully, but you *will* most certainly live with more fear and anxiety than you need to.

Your New Neighborhood

You're not down in the muck; you're not living any longer in the deadness of the world. Your environment is the presence of Christ, and you bring that environment with you wherever you go. That's why you're safe in a fallen world. As Jesus pointed out, you're *in* the world, but you're not *of* it (see John 17:14–18). You live among disobedient people, but you're not a disobedient person.

You're in the world, but it's not your true neighborhood; it's not where you live. You live in heavenly realms. You may find yourself on the ugliest streets of this fallen planet, but you're still in heavenly places in Christ Jesus. Jesus living in you positions you firmly in the heavenly neighborhood.

One of the most valuable things you can do as a Christian is to learn to live consciously in his presence. Remind yourself regularly, "Jesus Christ lives in me. I am in heavenly places now." That practice will save you a lot of aggravation, grumbling, and fear. It will also make you available for God's purposes wherever you find yourself.

Chapter 9: **TRANSFORMED** and **COURAGEOUS**

Do you work with people who are annoying and cross? Do you wish sometimes you could work with only pleasant people who talk nicely and smell good, complete all of their assignments, and never complain? People who never leave their work for you to do, who don't play political games to try to get one up on you, who don't keep dirty pictures in their lockers and in their minds?

The reason you're where you are is because Jesus loves the people there—and you are the way he loves them. If *you* don't love them, *he* can't. You're there not because you would choose it; you're there because you choose to be with him, and he has chosen to be there.

If you're going to be with Jesus, you're going to spend time with some difficult people, because he came to seek and to save that which was "lost" (see Luke 19:10). Feel free to cross out "lost" and substitute any of these words: ugly, mean, vulgar, immoral, dangerous, violent, abusive. Those adjectives describe the kinds of people Jesus came to find. And lo and behold, he found some right where you work! Isn't that remarkable? All he wants to do is love them, and you are the way he wants to love them.

> Remind yourself regularly, "Jesus Christ lives in me. I am in heavenly places now."

That doesn't mean you have to live where they live. You're in heavenly places. When you walk into the office, you're not down in the grime and dirt with them—that's not where you are. Everyone around you may be complaining and bellyaching, but what's happening where you live? There's a song being sung down inside you someplace. You don't even know all the words to it, but it sings itself in your mind. You think of a particular person, and you say a little prayer for them. There's a separate world going on within you. You're not detached or in a coma; but at the same time, in a very sane way, you're not a part of all the stuff that's happening around you.

Every once in a while, somebody will notice, and he or she will ask, "Where are you anyway? What's going on with you?" It won't happen all the time; but once in a while you'll get the opportunity to tell people about the world you live in and how Jesus Christ can help them.

Light in the Darkness

Ephesians 5:8 says, "For you were once darkness, but now you are light in the Lord." This verse doesn't say you were *in* darkness but that you *were* darkness. Before you were in Christ, wherever you went, you not only were dark, you made everything dark when you got there. You'd come into a good conversation, and it would be worse because you showed up. You were spreading darkness. But now you are light!

Think about it: you don't control light with darkness. When you leave a room, you don't turn the darkness on; you turn the lights off. You control darkness with light. Why? Because darkness has no substance; it's simply the absence of light. You can't measure dark waves. They don't exist.

In a very practical sense, then, you are where you are because Jesus wants to bring light to darkness. He wants to position himself beside hopeless people so they will sense hope. He wants to position himself beside angry people so they will sense peace. He

116

wants to position himself beside depressed people so they will experience joy. He honestly believes that every person is worth dying for, and he doesn't want them left alone in their chaos, whether they respond to him or not. You are one of the ways he stays within their reach—just in case they call on him to be saved.

A New Potential and a New Purpose

Ephesians 2:10 continues the description of who you are in your new life in Christ: "For we are God's workmanship, created in Christ Jesus to do good works, which God prepared in advance for us to do." Did you know you are a work of art? That's what *workmanship* means. The word is translated from the Greek term *poema*: a poem. You are God's masterpiece.

You may not think he's doing good work—but he thinks he's doing great work! You don't interrupt a master as he paints and instruct him, "You know, if you had only added a little more green to that area . . . made that section a little darker." You don't do that. If it looks good to him, it's good. Your opinion is irrelevant, because he is the master and you're not.

Artwork is a masterpiece the moment the master picks up the brush and puts the first line on canvas. It doesn't become a masterpiece when it's completed; it's already a masterpiece when it begins. Furthermore, it's not a masterpiece because of the subject matter. Regardless of the subject of the painting, it's a masterpiece because the master painted it. If Michelangelo drew a snail, it would be a masterpiece. Art collectors would pay millions for the original.

Don't look in the mirror or into the brokenness of your spirit and despise God's work. Don't get caught up in the kind of thinking that says, *I'm not everything I should be, but I'm working on it.* Your work is irrelevant, quite frankly, because you're not the master.

Someone once told me, "I'm a self-made man." He was a friend of mine, so I was free to be a bit of a smart aleck. "Well, the workmanship certainly shows," I said. "It's quite obvious who made you."

The fact that you are a work of art isn't about *you* doing well, it's about God doing well. Everything God does, he does well. When he finished creating the earth, he stepped back and admiringly declared, "It's good. Didn't I do a good job there?" And all of heaven said, "Boy, you really did." Nobody added, "Well, God, you know, if you just hadn't made that elephant's trunk quite so long."

You can have your opinion, but it doesn't change reality. God's opinion is the one that counts, because he's God. And his opinion always reflects reality. You may as well agree with his opinion about you and live in the real world!

Spiritual Progress

I'm not advocating passivity, but I would venture to say you are probably just about where you ought to be in your spiritual walk. Unless, of course, you're just fooling around and not taking God seriously. Being a nominal, playacting Christian is not fun; it's a miserable way to live. The only way to understand and experience full joy as a Christian is to seriously follow Jesus in every conceivable way and at every conceivable cost, 100 percent. Anything less is not worth the effort. A little bit of Christianity only makes you a miserable sinner. You're just holy enough to not enjoy sinning—not that you enjoyed it all that much before; sin's pleasure never lasts long. But now that you know what real joy is, why would you mess around with half-baked, lukewarm Christianity?

My guess, though, is that you're serious about following Jesus. Otherwise, why would you be spending your time reading this book? That means you're probably just about where you ought to be in your walk with God. You may not be as spiritual as your Uncle Jim, but you're probably about as spiritual as *you* should be. You may not be as holy as your spouse thinks you ought to be, but—while I'm sure you married a wonderful person—it's God's viewpoint that really matters.

Married people may be shocked to hear this: you are not your spouse's Holy Spirit. You can't "help along" the spiritual growth of your mate. Whenever I tried to work on my wife, she always had to recover from it, and God had to repair it. Time and time again God said, "Would you please keep your hands off what I'm trying to do? You don't have a clue what's going on here. Enjoy my masterpiece, but leave it alone." It's amazing how much better our marriage is, now that I've stopped tweaking God's work. Barb is his workmanship, his masterpiece, not mine.

Good Works

Look again at Ephesians 2:10, this time focusing on the second part of the verse: "For we are God's workmanship, *created in Christ Jesus to do good works, which God prepared in advance for us to do.*" Isn't it amazing? Two things are happening at once: first, God is creating you for specific good works; and second, he's creating specific good works for you. Both of these things are going on. A significant aspect of God's workmanship is to make *you* a craftsman, a master, who will do good works—not haphazardly, but artistically. This is where your potential and your purpose merge.

The "good works" are not pie-in-the-sky, huge, way-out-there projects. They are the things you do on a daily basis, the good works that present themselves opportunistically in your life. Helping someone in need, sharing joy with others, praying with someone who's hurting, spending time with a lonely person, responding compassionately—whatever comes to you in your day as an opportunity to do good, I can say to you categorically: That is a good work God has prepared in advance for you to do. It hasn't come to you accidentally.

> God has not only made you a masterpiece; he's made you an artist.

I can say to you further that you are, at that very moment, totally prepared not only to respond to the opportunity, but to do so artistically, masterfully. When God sees you, the way you respond, the way you help, he says, "Now there—that's the right way to do it. That's a work of art. Isn't that terrific? Haven't I done a good job? I've not only done a good job on that person, I can do a masterful job *through* that person."

God has not only made you a masterpiece; he's made you an artist. He's made you capable of responding masterfully whenever the opportunity arises to do a good work he's prepared for you. God knows that artistic ability is developed through instruction and practice. You can be sure his assignments will always be tailored to your development level.

That's why it's so terribly important for you not to despise who you are, what you're like, what you look like, what your capabilities are, what your IQ is, what your educational background is. God is fully capable of working in you in such a way that everything he has for you to do, you cannot only do well, you can do masterfully.

Do Today Well

There are many details I don't know about the day ahead when I arrive at my office in the morning, especially when I've just returned from traveling. As this is being written, I've been away from the office for ten days. Duties are accumulating on my desk and on my calendar. People are calling to make appointments with me; events are getting planned; speaking requests are coming in. When I return, my secretary will sort through everything, and some of these items will be put on my calendar. These will determine how my next period of time will be spent.

I've learned I can worry and wonder and call the office every day to ask, "What's going on? What do I need to know?" Or I can walk in on that first day back knowing I absolutely will be the person Jesus needs me to be to handle each calendar item in the coming weeks. It's not my job to be ready; it's his job to work in my life so that he has made me ready. My job is to respond to him.

I'm not a passive person. But I can't totally prepare for the future for one very simple reason: I don't know what the future is. It's hard to prepare for the unknown! I do have a plan, but my plan is not necessarily my future. Have you lived long enough to figure that out? There are plans, and there is the future—and sometimes they don't match.

Only God can prepare me for the future. Tomorrow has to come through today to get to me. So if I am with God today and I am responsive to him today, I will be prepared for the future he has for me tomorrow. If I do today well, I will be prepared for tomorrow.

That's why the Scripture commands, "Do not worry about tomorrow" (Matthew 6:34). You can't make yourself taller; you can't add any more hair to your head; there are things you simply can't do. Focus on what Christ desires for you today, and you'll be ready for tomorrow.

When individuals come to my office next week, I will hold hands with sadness and confusion and hurt. Some people will be there as a last resort. Some will be in a state of brokenness; they will cry and spill out their stories and their confessions. They will share with me their dreams and their pain. And unless Jesus Christ has worked in my life to prepare me for those moments, I will have nothing to offer except sympathy.

But if I understand I really am God's workmanship, that Christ is working in me and he is also working in them, and he has brought us together at precisely the right time, then I can, with confidence, care for them.

What will I do? Frankly, I will do what comes to my mind to do. I will simply follow the prompting of the Holy Spirit at that moment. I will say what I believe he wants me to say, and it will not be a struggle; it will be that which comes to my mouth easily. It will be the response that is naturally there.

So relax! If you want to minister effectively, don't get uptight; God really is working in you. Whatever he's given you to do today, he's designed you for it and it for you. That's why I'm going to be talking to those specific people next week rather than others. It's not coincidental; it's not because they couldn't get an appointment with someone else; it's by design. They are people God has prepared to talk to me, and he's prepared me to talk to them. When we come together, we are both reflecting the preparation of Jesus Christ in that meeting.

Comfortable in Your Own Skin

Can you transfer this concept into your life? Can you see the opportunities that come to you, however great or slight, were prepared for you and you for them? These opportunities fit you as you are, not as you try to be somebody else. If you can't accept yourself in Christ, if you're not comfortable with this person he's making you to be, you will lack the supply of confidence and courage necessary to effectively share his life with others.

"But what about my faults and sins?"

As to the nonsense still left in your life, you can be sure God's cleaning that up. Of course, there's always something to clean up! Cooperate with the work of the Holy Spirit in making you holy; but as you do, understand who you are is not only acceptable, it's essential. The way you respond; the way you talk; the expressions on your face; the way you smile, move, gesture; your sense of humor; the things you laugh at; the things you cry about; the tone of voice you use in certain circumstances—all of the specifics that make up who you are—all of these things are valuable in the assignments God sends. He has prepared specific good works for who you are. That means you need to be you.

A shy young woman came to talk with me because she was frightened by the direction she was getting from the Lord. The thing that made her so delightful as she sat in my office was that she was just herself. She was scared. "I'm scared to death!" she said. "I don't even know why I'm telling you this."

What she didn't realize was that it was her very reticence, that very quality of her personality she abhorred, that made her attractive, safe, and trustworthy to others. She'd come to me to get rid of the fear.

"My dear, if we get rid of the fear, we get rid of you," I told her. "We can deal with the phobia; you don't have to lie awake nights in terror. But one of the reasons people are responding to you is because you're *not* coming on as a slick paper professional. You're coming on as scared to death, and a lot of people are listening to you because they're scared too. That's OK."

Can you be comfortable with yourself as you are, filled with him? And can you be comfortable with the fact that if you're doing things that displease him, he'll tell you? You need to have an agreement between you and God that says, "If you tell me, Lord, I'll do something about it. If there is something about me blocking your ministry through my life, please tell me. I'm not looking to see how much I can get away with; if it needs to be cleaned up, I'm willing." Then relax in who you are and who he is leading you to become.

You may say, "Well, I'm just not very social."

Then don't be social. It's OK; he can work with that. If Jesus wants you to be more outgoing, he'll put you in situations that will develop social skills. Don't let your reserve be an excuse to withdraw. Instead, acknowledge his presence in your life and work confidently wherever he takes you.

Weak and Strong

"Uncle Bud" Robinson was the founder of the revival movement that became the Church of the Nazarene. He was a great preacher who held crusades all across America around the turn of the twentieth century. Remarkably, Bud Robinson had a speech impediment. He stammered so terribly that people would have to strain to understand him. Yet thousands of people who listened to his messages gave their lives to Christ, and the results of his ministry continue today.

Like Uncle Bud, you will minister not because of your strengths or weaknesses, but because of who you are in Christ. Each of us is both strong and weak at the same time. So relax! Whatever comes to you today, you have been utterly prepared to respond in an artistic fashion. You are a ministering work of art. The way you would do it is the way God wants it done. And responding to his leading today will prepare you for tomorrow.

Here is a true statement you can make to yourself as you begin each day: "I am God's workmanship, created in Christ Jesus to do good works, which God prepared in advance for me to do." And a true prayer you can pray: "Lord, today I want to be alert to the good works you have *designed me for* and that you have *designed for me*. Help me to go about my day aware of your presence. I welcome your masterful work in my life; I accept it and rejoice in it!"

You are God's masterpiece. Believe it!

WELCOME
to the
FAMILY

To me, one of the most marvelous descriptions in the book of Revelation is that of great multitudes of people from all nations and all tongues praising the Lord together (see Revelation 7:9–10). I've had the privilege of traveling in many regions of the world— some quite civilized and some quite primitive—and I've had a tiny glimpse of this picture.

A friend of mine, Jack Hayford, wrote the magnificent, now-international hymn, "Majesty, Worship His Majesty." I've stood with former cannibals in New Guinea singing, "Majesty, worship his majesty." I've sat in Japan singing "Majesty." I've been in Australia, New Zealand, Europe; even in Croatia following a divisive war, singing "Majesty, worship his majesty," with Serbs, Bosnians, and Croatians together.

What a time it will be when we are all together in heaven and we are singing! (Those of us who can only sing in English are a minority, you know. Most people in the world can sing "Majesty" in four or five languages.) I'll sing in English, but that will be fine; it will blend. All of us who are in Christ—whatever our color; whatever our nation, race, language, or dialect; whatever our background—are the people of the New Covenant. What an incredible truth! Yet, this "international" implication of the gospel was not understood at first, nor was it accepted easily.

A Perilous Assignment

Paul is called "the apostle to the Gentiles" (Romans 11:13). He was the person the Holy Spirit chose to bring the message of Christ to those outside the Jewish nation. When Paul said yes to the Lord on the road to Damascus, he was saying yes to a dangerous assignment, one that would lead to martyrdom.

You and I were that assignment.

Paul proclaimed that Jesus was not only a national Messiah, but the universal Savior. That message gives me hope—but the man who brought the message on my behalf paid with his life. So when I come to this next part of Ephesians 2, I do so with a great degree of awe and gratitude in my heart.

Those of us who are Gentiles owe a debt of eternal love to this man, because it is his message that brought us hope in Jesus. And it was this message which forced Paul to spend much of his ministry life in prison. He was attacked, stoned, and beaten numerous times. And he always came out of those prisons and beatings declaring exactly the same message.

Ephesians 2 contains the heart of that vital message: "Jesus Christ is *your* Messiah. He is *your* Savior." Gentiles are invited to know God!

Chapter 10: WELCOME to the FAMILY

Israel: The People of God

It is sometimes forgotten that God did, in fact, call Israel into existence; he did come to Abraham; he did make a promise; he did start a nation in Abraham. He established a covenant with Israel—the beginning point of his revelation of himself to the world. That covenant will, in fact, be fully kept and fully completed.

But when the Messiah arrived, the revolutionary news was that he was not only the national Messiah of Israel. Something bigger was going on. In the Gospels, if you read carefully the things Jesus said and did and the questions the Pharisees asked him, you begin to realize the extreme animosity that sprang up around this "something bigger."

The covenant, which made the people of Israel uniquely the people of God, was about to be completed. It would be expanded into a new covenant that would include all nations. A way was being made for noncovenant people to come into the presence of God and enjoy the status and blessings of the people of God. To the religious leaders of the time, this concept was an unthinkable blasphemy. They killed Jesus at the announcement of it, and they killed Paul for proclaiming it.

In the church at Ephesus, many believers came from a non-Jewish background. So it was appropriate, even necessary, for Paul to explain their place, their relationship, in this mixed-race church. How was it possible that Jews and Gentiles could now belong in one family?

Ephesians 2:11–12 begins: "Therefore, remember that formerly you who are Gentiles by birth and called 'uncircumcised' by those who call themselves 'the circumcision' (that done in the body by the hands of men)—remember that at that time you were separate from Christ, excluded from citizenship in Israel and foreigners to the covenants of the promise, without hope and without God in the world."

As Gentiles you and I were outside the national covenant God made with Israel. This separation and alienation had nothing to do with our sinfulness; it had to do with our national identity. We were not part of the people with whom God made a covenant, and there was no way we could experience the benefits of that covenant. So we were without God and without hope.

God's decision to make a covenant with Israel did nothing for us. The covenant of the Old Testament is not a covenant with those of us who are Gentiles. That's what Paul is saying—the covenant is great, the promises are great, but we were not part of it. We were excluded from the covenant, because we are not Israelites.

A New Nation

Then comes this wonderful phrase in verse 13: "But now . . ." Isn't that huge? Something has universally changed. "But now in Christ Jesus . . ."

Could it be? Maybe this Messiah, this Jesus, transcends the national barrier. Maybe there's a way for us to be connected, not just to Israel, but to God. Maybe there's hope for us after all!

Verses 13–15 go on: "But now in Christ Jesus you who once were far away have been brought near through the blood of Christ. For he himself is our peace, who has made the two one"—he has brought the Jews and the Gentiles together—"and has destroyed the barrier, the dividing wall of hostility"—that is, the national barrier, the wall of hostility that has separated those of us who are

Gentiles from the covenant. He has done this "by abolishing in his flesh the law with its commandments and regulations." In other words, Jesus fulfilled the covenant. He accomplished all that the law and the commandments required.

It's a simple truth: law exists because there are lawbreakers. When the law is fulfilled, the need for the law is gone. When there are no longer lawbreakers, there is no longer a need for the law.

Jesus came to earth and through his obedience fulfilled the Law. He obeyed fully and completely, not just for an historical thirty-three-and-a-half years, but through his death and resurrection too. He was the Lamb of God "slain from the foundation of the world" (Revelation 13:8 NKJV). He transcended history. Because that's true, there is no longer a lawbreaker, but a law-fulfiller. The Law has been fulfilled in Jesus, so the need for the Law is gone.

> **His obedience is the basis of our salvation.**

Now hearts can be so changed through a relationship with God in Christ that we are able to simply obey one law—the one that Jesus established, the law of love. No other laws are necessary. In that sense, Jesus "abolished the law." He did it on our behalf. Now *his* obedience is the basis of *our* salvation. It's his obedience that gives us hope and access to God.

Verse 15 continues, "His purpose was to create in himself one new man out of the two, thus making peace." By "one new man," Paul wasn't talking about an "adjusted" person—he was talking about a totally new creation. Jew plus Gentile plus Jesus equals a new creation. It's incredible! Jesus doesn't make Gentiles out of Israelites, and he doesn't make Israelites out of Gentiles. He takes the two of them, redeems them together, and makes an entirely new race.

Then he reconciles that new race to God: "And in this one body to reconcile both of them to God through the cross, by which he put to death their hostility. He came and preached peace to you who were far away and peace to those who were near" (vv. 16–17). He preached the same thing to both Gentiles and Jews, and the next verse encapsulates that message: "For through him we both have access to the Father by one Spirit."

That's almost too good to be true, isn't it? It almost sounds like a sci-fi story! But it is, indeed, the truth. And the result is this: "Consequently, you are no longer foreigners and aliens, but fellow citizens with God's people and members of God's household" (v. 19).

Now you and I are covenant people!

Included in the Promises

I was a university student when this truth caught hold of me. I had rented a room in a large house owned by a Swedish matron, Ma Sedonquist. Ma had a dog named Ginger who often came up to my room. Sometimes she'd holler up the stairs, "Yerry, have you seen Yinyer?" The first time she did that, I fell off my bed laughing. I had to put my books away; my concentration was gone.

For twenty-five dollars a month, I got the room and all the coffee I could drink. The problem with Ma's coffee was that she brewed it in a huge Pyrex pot and left it on a hot plate early in the morning. By late afternoon (which is when she usually offered me a cup) you couldn't swallow it; you had to chew it. One drink could keep you awake for three days—which can be a good thing if you're in college. It was probably the reason I was awake and reading my Bible that particular day.

I remember sitting by my bed, reading this section of Ephesians. And all of a sudden it hit me: *I'm a covenant person. And if I'm a covenant person, then everything God ever said to any of his covenant people is also true for me!*

Somehow along the way, I'd picked up the suspicion that parts of the Bible were not intended for me. *Those* promises were for the Jews, and *those* were for the folks in the Old Testament, and *these* were for the apostles. I was left with John 3:16, a little bit of Romans, and the whole book of Revelation, which I couldn't understand!

But, if I had become an heir of the covenant promises, then all of the Scripture was mine. It didn't matter where it was in the Bible; it was mine. I thought, *Whoa! That's really good!* I remember going back through my Bible, excited and happy as I reread God's promises and noted, *Now, that's for me! That's mine.*

It wasn't that I had a religious experience; it was that I suddenly understood something that is true: under the New Covenant, I, a non-Israeli, am fully included in the people of God. And so are you.

It doesn't matter what color we are, what ethnic background we have, or what language we speak. We are not second-rate citizens, as if Jesus tweaks us just enough to become semi-Israelis. We are a *new* creation. There's a new race here. Jesus takes the Jews and the Gentiles (and who else is there? You're either a Jew or you're not, and the "nots" are called Gentiles), and he makes a new race of people. Then he reconciles that new race of people to God, based upon his obedience, his sacrifice, his death, and his resurrection—motivated by his love for all of us.

A New Temple

Verses 19–20 continue, "Consequently, you are no longer foreigners and aliens, but fellow citizens with God's people and members of God's household, built on the foundation of the apostles and prophets, with Christ Jesus himself as the chief cornerstone."

Jesus, you see, is the meeting place. The apostles, the prophets, the Jews, the Gentiles—how does God bring them together? He makes Jesus the cornerstone of the building. That's where they meet.

Verse 21: "In him the whole building is joined together and rises to become a holy temple in the Lord." You have to understand, the temple was a sacred, holy place for the Jews, a beautiful architectural structure located on a mountain. Paul is treading on risky ground here by proclaiming a new temple. In his day that was a very dangerous thing to say.

Verse 22 continues: "And in him you too are being built together to become a dwelling in which God lives by his Spirit." The implications of this statement are profound. The old physical temple is no longer relevant in God's system. The real temple of God is now a collection of redeemed people—the new race. God has come to dwell not in temples made with hands, but in the hearts of his redeemed, reconciled, newly created race. The Old Testament temple has been replaced with a New Testament church!

Do you see why Paul lost his life? Years earlier, when the

Chapter 10: WELCOME to the FAMILY

Pharisees listened to Jesus, they looked toward the future. "If people start believing this, we're done," they said to one another. "It's the end of all we've lived for and all we believe—the end of our system." Do you see why, in their minds, Jesus had to die? And why, later on, the people who killed Jesus used the same reasoning to kill Paul?

The Mystery

Ephesians 3 opens with a reminder from Paul to those of us who are Gentiles: *We're* the reason he is an apostle. He was specifically commissioned by God to bring us this amazing message:

> For this reason I, Paul, the prisoner of Christ Jesus for the sake of you Gentiles—
>
> Surely you have heard about the administration of God's grace that was given to me for you, that is, the mystery made known to me by revelation, as I have already written briefly. In reading this, then, you will be able to understand my insight into the mystery of Christ, which was not made known to men in other generations as it has now been revealed by the Spirit to God's holy apostles and prophets. This mystery is that through the gospel the Gentiles are heirs together with Israel, members together of one body, and sharers together in the promise in Christ Jesus. (vv. 1–6)

The mystery, the secret, is that Jesus was not a national Messiah; he was a universal Savior! That's a concise summary of Paul's message and life passion. He continues in verses 7–12:

> I became a servant of this gospel by the gift of God's grace given me through the working of his power. Although I am

less than the least of all God's people, this grace was given me: to preach to the Gentiles the unsearchable riches of Christ, and to make plain to everyone the administration of this mystery, which for ages past was kept hidden in God, who created all things. His intent was that now, through the church, the manifold wisdom of God should be made known to the rulers and authorities in the heavenly realms, according to his eternal purpose which he accomplished in Christ Jesus our Lord. In him and through faith in him we may approach God with freedom and confidence.

This is the gospel; this is the message; this is the proclamation of the church: we can approach God with freedom and confidence, not because we've had a good day; not because we've done well; but because Jesus has done well. It's all because of Jesus! Even on our worst day, we are still God's covenant people *in him*. Incredible!

Paul's Second Prayer

Passionately issuing out of the declarations we just read, Paul then prays a prayer that could only come from a loving and courageous heart. As recorded in Ephesians 3:13–19, it is the second great prayer in Paul's letter to the Ephesians, inspired by the Holy Spirit for the church in all ages:

> I ask you, therefore, not to be discouraged because of my sufferings for you, which are your glory.
>
> For this reason I kneel before the Father, from whom his whole family in heaven and on earth derives its name. I pray that out of his glorious riches he may strengthen you with power through his Spirit in your inner being, so that Christ

may dwell in your hearts through faith. And I pray that you, being rooted and established in love, may have power, together with all the saints, to grasp how wide and long and high and deep is the love of Christ, and to know this love that surpasses knowledge—that you may be filled to the measure of all the fullness of God.

What a wonderful prayer! And what about that last sentence? Can you imagine being "filled to the measure of all the fullness of God"? That's a huge statement!

Verses 20–21: "Now to him who is able to do immeasurably more than all we ask or imagine, according to his power that is at work within us, to him be glory in the church and in Christ Jesus throughout all generations, for ever and ever! Amen."

Notice Paul doesn't just say, "to him who is able to do great things." He says, "to him who is able to do immeasurably more." And not just "immeasurably more," but "immeasurably more than all we ask." And not just "immeasurably more than all we ask," but "immeasurably more than all we ask *or imagine.*" God's power and glory just keep going. Throughout how many generations? "All generations." Does that include us? Does that reach the baby boomers, the Gen-X-ers? Absolutely. It's God's clear intention that he is glorified in his people in all generations forever and ever!

Unlimited Access

When you're going through a difficult time or a period of doubt or questioning, I recommend you take a few minutes each morning and write down one thing that is true for you that day because you're a covenant person. For example, you're a child of promise. You have access to God. You don't need to go through intermediaries. Without disrespect to anyone's background or tradition, you no longer need to approach God through a saint or the Mother of Jesus or a church official or a priest. You are welcome, just as you are, to come directly into the presence of God himself.

No one can pray better than you can. Someone else may use grander words, but God has a way of reaching past the words and capturing the message of the heart. Use your own words—or no words at all; in his presence you're not limited to your vocabulary.

Sometimes I forget this, and I catch myself apologizing, "Jesus, this is a pitiful prayer. I don't know how to say what I'm trying to say." Even with the assistance of the Holy Spirit, there are times when I feel, *God, I'm just not a very good pray-er.* At other times I catch myself spinning up a flowery, impressive-sounding prayer, and I think, *Why are you doing this? Who are you talking to here? Is God going to be impressed with your mastery of the English language?*

You don't need big words or rituals or incense or anything else to pray. Because you are a covenant person, God looks past such things and answers directly to your heart.

At Home with the Father

As a covenant child of God, you can do what even the high priest could not do under the Old Covenant. You can, without fear, *re-side* in God's presence. Not just visit the Holy of Holies once a year with fear and trembling, bringing a sacrifice you hope has been prepared properly; with a rope tied around your ankle, so that if the sacrifice doesn't work, the other priests can pull your body out. No, you can come into everything the Holy of Holies represented—into the very presence of God—without fear, hesitation, or pretense. Not only can you go there, you live there; it's your address.

"What's your address?"

"It's the Holy of Holies." (That's another way of saying "in Christ" or "in his presence.")

"Well, now. Just who do you think you are?"

"I'm a covenant child of God."

"But aren't you afraid?"

"No, I'm less afraid of God than many children are of their earthly fathers. I'm welcome there."

My kids never knock when they come home. They just burst in the front door: "Hey, anybody home?" When I go to my daughter's house, I walk right in and call, "Hey, I'm here." We're family; we're welcome.

The Scripture says you can now, without fear, come into the presence of God and say, "Abba, Father!" If you lived in a Jewish home, that's what you'd hear. The father would come home at night and the little children would clamor, "Abba! Daddy!" It's a term of endearment. "This is my papa, my daddy." My wife and her sisters still call their ninety-six-year-old father Daddy. Even in heaven his name will probably be Daddy!

> **You can, without fear, *reside* in God's presence.**

Let me encourage you: Take some time each day to think about your status as a covenant child of God. Stop what you're doing periodically, and allow the implications to seep into your awareness. Remind yourself—maybe when you're brushing your teeth; maybe when you're driving to work; maybe when you're saying the prayer before the evening meal: "I'm a covenant child of God. I'm in the family." The world we live in can cause you to forget who you are, and you will begin to live as though you are still of the other race—the alienated one. The truth is, you're in the family that has been reconciled to God.

Doubting the Doubts

I'm not telling you to make up pretty little affirmations to repeat, so you'll feel better about yourself. *You are a covenant child of God.* That's the reality. It's true. It's infinitely truer than any of your doubts about it! When you doubt, you have two choices: you can believe the doubt or doubt the doubt. My suggestion is that when you're faced with a doubt about who you are in Christ, doubt it!

For example: "God is not pleased with me today."

"I doubt that. I'll bet he is. I believe he is pleased with me today."

Or, "I don't know if the Holy Spirit really lives in me or not."

"I doubt that. In fact, I know he does."

You are a covenant child of God. That's who you are. Not because of anything you've ever done or ever will do, but because God sent his Son, Jesus, to fulfill all the requirements of the Old Covenant and usher in the New Covenant, bringing Jew and Gentile together in a new creation.

"To him be glory in the church and in Christ Jesus throughout all generations, for ever and ever!"

Amen!

HOW YOU LIVE

A WORTHY LIFE

Paul's letters are almost always set up in two sections. First, he explains the theological and philosophical facts. Then he turns to practical application. After developing the theology, he says, "Since this is true, here's what ought to be taking place as you go about your day." Or as one renowned author put it, "How should we then live?"[1]

Ephesians 4:1 begins the transition: "As a prisoner for the Lord, then, I urge you to live a life worthy of the calling you have received." What calling? The one Paul described in the first three chapters of Ephesians. As a believer in Christ, you've been called to a new identity, a new purpose, and a new mission. You've been called to be a covenant person; the living temple where God now lives; light in the world. That's who you are. Now he admonishes: live like the person you have just understood yourself to be! To the question, "How should we then live?" he answers, "Live a life worthy of your calling. Live out your new life in Christ."

Part 4: **HOW YOU LIVE**

Paul then begins to build a list of what that new life should include: "Be completely humble and gentle; be patient, bearing with one another in love" (v. 2). Because of your calling, genuine humility is now possible; gentleness is possible; patience is possible; so is bearing with others in love. Those are things you may have always wanted to do but struggled to accomplish before. Now as part of a new race of people, that's the way you live. You can do it now. It's not so much a command as it is an invitation: Be who you really are. Make the choice.

But what exactly does the word *humility* mean? You can't choose to be humble if you don't have a working definition for it. What does the word *gentle* mean? What does *patience* mean? *Love*? Unless you have definitions for these qualities, you won't understand what you are capable of doing. Here are working definitions that help me:

- Humility: holding an accurate view of yourself, using God's opinion as the standard of measurement

- Gentleness: quiet and peaceful strength

- Patience: being at peace with God's agenda and with his schedule for growth in your life and in the lives of those around you

- Love: choosing to act for another person's highest good

Paul then goes on: "Make every effort to keep the unity of the Spirit through the bond of peace. There is one body and one Spirit—just as you were called to one hope when you were called—one Lord, one faith, one baptism; one God and Father of all, who is over all and through all and in all" (vv. 3–6). In these verses he is naming the seven unifying points of the Christian faith:

- One body

- One Spirit

- One hope

- One Lord

- One faith

- One baptism

- One God and Father of all

These are essential tenets for believers of all creeds, labels, and distinctions. If you lose your conviction on any one of these points, you cease to be Christian.

Gifts for the Church

Ephesians 4:7–12 continues:

> But to each one of us grace has been given as Christ apportioned it. This is why it says:
> "When he ascended on high,
> he led captives in his train
> and gave gifts to men."
> (What does "he ascended" mean except that he also descended to the lower, earthly regions? He who descended is the very one who ascended higher than all the heavens, in order to fill the whole universe.) It was he who gave some to be apostles, some to be prophets, some to be evangelists, and

some to be pastors and teachers, to prepare God's people for works of service.

Apostles, prophets, evangelists, pastors, and teachers—these are gifts, presents, like you'd give at a birthday party. They are not deserved or earned; they are simply given to bless. In fact, Jesus gave these presents to the church for a specific purpose: to prepare God's new race, his covenant people, for works of service. That's what apostles, prophets, evangelists, pastors, and teachers do. They have different functions but basically the same job description: they prepare God's people for works of service.

Let's look at the specific function of each one.

The Gift of Apostles

Apostles are not given to do the work of the ministry but to help prepare God's people to do the work of ministry. The ministry of this body of people, this church, is done *by the people*. In the old system it was done by the professionals (the Jewish priests) because only the professionals had access to God. The ministers ministered on behalf of the congregation. The elite class acted for all the rest.

That is no longer the case. Because of Christ, the barrier that separated you from God is gone, and you have equal access with the professionals into the Father's direct presence. So do I. There is no longer an elite class needed to minister to God on our behalf or to minister to us on behalf of God. What a marvelous change! It restructures everything.

The gift of apostolic ministry prepares God's people so the people themselves can do the work of the ministry. We can do the work. It's possible now because we are covenant people. We are in Christ.

Chapter 11: A WORTHY LIFE

The Gift of Prophets

The role of prophecy is radically different under the New Covenant than it was under the Old Covenant. It still exists, but it's very different now. Before, prophets heard from God and then shared his word with the people. Today that's not necessary. Prophets are not here to get God's word for you, *because you can get God's word for yourself.* You don't need a professional to tell you what God is saying to you. Why not? Because he lives in you. Listen. His voice is available to you.

Be careful when people come into your life and give you "a word from the Lord." Unless that word from the Lord agrees with what the Lord is already saying to you, suspend it. Wait and see. God delivers his own messages now, and he knows your name and address.

"Well," you say, "that sounds pretty dangerous. How can I be sure I'm hearing God's voice correctly?"

Actually, the real danger is letting someone else be God's voice to you. I'm not pleading for a kind of harsh individualism. The fact that we all have access to God doesn't do away with prophecy, but it does change the intent and the purpose of prophecy. A prophecy spoken by another person can be personally confirming, but prophet is an office we all share. We are a community of prophetic people.

Whatever else prophets do, whatever else they accomplish through prophecy, under the New Covenant their first and foremost goal is to prepare God's people for works of service. It's not that we hire them to come and speak God's word to us. Their purpose is not to tell us things we're capable of hearing on our own; rather, it's to help enable us to hear, see, and speak from God's perspective. Their job is to help us be prophetic people who can minister in our world.

The Gift of Evangelists

Evangelists are like prophets in the same sense. An evangelist is not a person who has the assignment of making converts. Yes, some people are especially gifted in expressing the gospel; but because we have applied the term *evangelist* to a professional function, we've misunderstood it. Evangelists are people who help the church—you and me—understand how Christ can be communicated in a way people will respond to him. They are given to equip the people of God, to provide the people of God with an evangelistic presence in their world.

The Gift of Pastors and Teachers

Unfortunately, we have made the term *pastor* so exclusive, so professionalized, that we think of pastors as those who work within and draw their paycheck from a religious organization. We think of them as people we pay to watch over us—to care for our needs and provide for our spiritual growth. We fail to understand we're all called to be what I call "cultural pastors"—people who act pastorally in the world, who minister to, care for, and love the people God has placed around them.

Jesus Christ came as the Great Shepherd, as a pastor to the world. That's what the word *pastor* means: shepherd. And if he is our model, then each of us is in the position of shepherding, or pastoring, the world in which he's strategically placed us. That means *you* are a pastor, whether you're in your home, in your community, at your school, in your office, or at your workbench.

Chapter 11: A WORTHY LIFE

Use Words When Necessary

People with the gift of pastoring equip the believers in their flocks to be pastors to the people around *them*. That means pastors are not only shepherds; they're teachers too. The pastor-teacher gift is really a single role. People who pastor give insight into Christ's teachings and help people apply the principles of Christ's life to their own.

Of course, teaching must be understood as much broader than formal classroom instruction or sermon presentation. Cultural pastors do not necessarily teach out loud. As Saint Francis of Assisi famously said, "Preach the gospel at all times. Use words when necessary."

I love to fly-fish for trout on mountain streams and high lakes. I read books about fly-fishing. I tie my flies. I build my rods. I am a hopeless addict. Fly-fishing has been part of my life since I was a small boy growing up in the mountains of Montana and Idaho.

My hero was my Uncle Harold. In my young mind he was the greatest fisherman who ever lived. He took me fishing with him when I was just a seven-year-old boy. I remember watching everything he did—how he spotted the fish; studied the water; tied the fly on the leader; cast with that big bamboo rod; stood behind a bush and watched to see if a fish would take the bait. I went home, found a long stick, and went through the entire exercise, catching fish after fish in the stream of my young imagination.

The day finally came when I was given my grandfather's bamboo rod (it proudly hangs on the wall of my den). I went down to the train yard in our little town and fished on Spring Creek. I will never forget the massive fight I had with that huge eight-inch trout. All the fish I have caught since have never quite measured up to that one.

I always tell people, "My Uncle Harold taught me to fish." I don't ever remember him saying much, but he sure was a good teacher.

A Cultural Pastor

I suppose one of the things I loved most about my father was that he was one of the most effective cultural pastors I've ever met. At the same time, he was probably one of the least effective professional ones.

Raised on a Montana farm, Milt Cook quit school before finishing the eighth grade to get a job. As a young construction worker wanting to improve his prospects, he saved enough money to order some welding instruction books from a correspondence school. He never had enough money to continue the course beyond the first two books. But he read those two, and at the age of twenty-two, he hired on as a welder in Wallace, Idaho.

Wallace was a busy mining town, where there was always machinery breaking down and in need of welding. Of course, Dad hadn't been on the job three minutes before his employers realized he wasn't a real welder, but his raw nerve impressed the shop owners. They decided, "Well, if he wants to be a welder, we'll just make a welder out of him."

Those men were old-school welders, and they taught young Milt far more than the basics. He learned how to lay out a design on the floor with a piece of chalk, weld the thing together, then go out into the field and bolt it up without needing to make even one adjustment. Eventually, Dad could do with a torch what carpenters couldn't do with a hammer, nails, and saw. Years later he jokingly told me, "If I could build houses out of steel, I could build a beautiful house. Too bad there's not much need for that!"

Chapter 11: A WORTHY LIFE

When Dad became a Christian in the early 1940s, the common thinking was that to serve God, you had to go to Bible college and become a pastor. Well, Milt Cook wanted to serve God, so he sold his house, quit his job, and moved to Los Angeles just at the end of World War II to pursue a ministry degree.

Once in California, he looked for work in the shipyards and got a job as a first-class burner, burning steel plate to repair warships. He had never done that sort of thing before, but it was the only job immediately available, and he had a family to support. For the first week he mainly burned himself. He came home every day seriously scorched, until a coworker finally taught him how to do the job safely.

After working the day shift at the shipyard, Milt would ride the streetcar to night school, using the trip back and forth for study. As a seven- and eight-year-old boy, I'd hear him come home well after midnight to drop into his bed,

> **I don't ever remember him saying much, but he sure was a good teacher.**

and I'd hear him rising early to go to work. He did that for four years, because he believed God wanted him to be a pastor.

Finally, degree in hand, he was sent to a remote mountain town in Colorado. The first winter we were there, the temperature fell to fifty-five degrees below zero. I didn't know human beings could live at that temperature! The church had been dissipated by a series of damaging circumstances, and few people remained. But Dad faithfully rose every Sunday and did what he knew to do: preach to three or four people and a bunch of empty seats.

There was no money for his salary, so the small congregation donated potatoes, their most plentiful crop. Again he worked as a welder, but work—and wages—were scarce. Finally, he collected enough money to put Mom on a bus and send her to her family in Spokane. Next, I sold newspapers, and Dad worked enough hours to buy an old car. We fixed it up and drove it to Washington, leaving behind the cold, the near-starvation, and the still-empty pews. As we reached the outskirts of Spokane, the bearings we'd put in the old car fell out. We hobbled into town, feeling as if we'd been delivered just in the nick of time.

Despite that experience, Dad persevered and went on to pastor three or four small churches. He loved the people; but he was a shy man, and it wasn't easy for him to stand up and preach. It was difficult, too, for him to sustain a long-term teaching ministry. As a result, his professional pastoral experiences were taxing and often discouraging.

Eventually, he returned to steel fabrication. I had become a pastor, and he set up shop in the area where my wife and I were pastoring. For many happy years he and Mom were part of our church. He served on the church council and the board of elders. He was a great blessing to me and to all the people.

One day when we were having lunch together, Dad said to me with tears in his eyes, "I don't know what's wrong with me. I know God called me to be a pastor, but I feel like I've disappointed him. I can't do what he asked me to do."

I began to ask some questions. For several years Dad had taught welding at the university in Anchorage, Alaska. Most of his students were in the military, because the local air force base sent them to Dad's classes for training. Besides teaching welding,

Dad often led these men to the Lord and ended up counseling and praying with them and their families.

"Dad, how many people would you figure you ministered to up there?" I asked.

"Well, there was Bob and Tom and Evelyn and Bill . . ."

"And where you're at now, is there any ministry going on with people there?"

"Oh man, you know . . ." And he started telling me about all the people he was helping through his business. One guy wanted him to come over on Thursday night and meet with his family. Someone else wanted him to teach a weekly Bible study in his home. Then there was Joe, an ex-convict Dad employed, who had been stealing from the business. Feeling guilty, Joe came to Dad to repent. He sat down, started bawling, and Dad led him to Jesus.

"Dad, hello!" I said. "You touch more of a congregation from your workbench than you ever preached to as a professional. All this time you've been thinking you failed him, Jesus has been fulfilling his call through you."

Dad brightened up, blew his nose, and said, "Well, that's a relief!" Then he stood up, paid his check, and went back to work.

Over the years Dad's pastoral ministry touched hundreds of people. Eternity alone will tell how great was the ripple effect of this one man responding to God's call to pastor and teach lost sheep from his welding shop.

The Benefits of Ministering

There are tremendous benefits that result when the people of God do the work of the ministry. And in fact, these benefits aren't realized *unless* the people of God do the work of the ministry. The first benefit is mentioned in Ephesians 4:12: "so that the body of Christ may be built up." The only way the body of Christ can be strengthened is if it is ministering. That is to say, the only way *you* can become strong is if *you*, as a part of the body of Christ, are ministering. There's no other way.

My youngest son lifts weights. When he was a college athlete, he was required to work out year-round, and he still continues that regimen. Once in a while I go to the gym with him. As I sit on a bench watching him lift, I feel so strong. I come out of there feeling healthy and powerful.

But a strange thing is happening: his muscles are getting harder, and I'm still flabby. Why? Because you don't get in shape by watching people lift weights. You don't get in shape by reading books about lifting weights. You get in shape by lifting weights. As a Christian you're not going to grow by listening to speakers, reading Christian books, or even attending church; you're going to grow by lifting the weights of ministry.

My son has fewer health problems than I do, partly because he's younger, but also because he's in good shape. We went fishing the other day, and I noticed he can walk up the long side of a cliff without getting tired. His legs are like tree trunks. I take four steps and ask, "Son, could we take a little break here? I'd like to sit on a rock and have a cup of coffee."

It's common knowledge that if you do the work of getting in shape, you'll have fewer health problems. It's my observation that the same principle applies to the church. Churches where a large proportion of the people are ministering are churches that are vital, healthy, and growing. And on an individual basis, ministering people seem to have a lot fewer personal problems than people who sit around and wait to be ministered to.

Another benefit that comes when the people of God do the work of the ministry is that "we all reach unity in the faith and in the knowledge of the Son of God" (v. 13). Unity comes from ministry—not from having the right pastor, the right church structure, or even doctrine that matches on every minor point. Spiritual maturity also comes from ministry. Verse 13 goes on to say that when you minister, you "become mature, attaining to the whole measure of the fullness of Christ."

Paul continues, "Then we will no longer be infants, tossed back and forth by the waves, and blown here and there by every wind of teaching and by the cunning and craftiness of men in their deceitful scheming" (v. 14). When you're busy with ministry, you don't tend to get caught up in silly theological fads. You simply don't have time for it. Ministering purifies your theology and keeps you away from flashy heresies.

> As a Christian you're going to grow by lifting the weights of ministry.

"Instead, speaking the truth in love, we will in all things grow up into him who is the Head, that is, Christ. From him the whole body, joined and held together by every supporting ligament, grows and builds itself up in love, as each part does its work" (vv. 15–16). Everybody has to be involved; each of us must do our part. The church is only as strong as its ministering core; it is not as strong as its attendance. You may have an attendance of five hundred and a ministering core of twenty-five. That makes you, in actuality, a church of twenty-five.

But what if everyone did get involved? What if all of us who are the church—the new race, the covenant people of God—did the work of the ministry, rather than leaving it to the professionals? According to these verses in Ephesians:

1. The body of Christ would be made strong.

2. Each of us, as individual members of that body, would be built up.

3. Churches would have fewer problems.

4. Individuals would have fewer personal problems.

5. We would reach unity in the faith; we'd have less divisiveness and fewer internal power struggles.

6. We'd become spiritually mature.

7. We'd stay on track theologically. Our beliefs would remain pure and sensible.

8. We would be less vulnerable to deception and other fraudulent practices by those people who try to profit, financially or otherwise, from the gospel.

You see, a church in which the people of God, and not just the paid staff, are doing the work of the ministry is a church that is more than a Sunday church. Ephesians 4 is not a picture of the church on Sunday. It's a picture of the church on Monday.

When you and I do the work of the ministry—that's when we become, together, the Monday morning church.

The CHRISTIAN LIFESTYLE

In the last chapter we saw that living a life worthy of our calling includes developing life habits such as humility, gentleness, and patience. It includes ministering to others. As Paul continues his letter to the Ephesians, he explains the Christian lifestyle further, encouraging believers to fully embrace their new identity in Christ.

What does it mean to embrace your new identity? As Paul describes it in Ephesians 4:17–32, it involves three basic steps:

1. Putting off your old identity

2. Allowing yourself to be made new in your attitudes and thoughts

3. Putting on your new self

Verse 17 begins with this admonition: "So I tell you this, and insist on it in the Lord, that you must no longer live as the Gentiles do, in the futility of their thinking." (For the Ephesian Christians the word *Gentile* had come to have new meaning. It applied not to those who were non-Jewish, but to those who were outside the New Covenant.)

Paul goes on to explain that these Gentiles "are darkened in their understanding and separated from the life of God because of the ignorance that is in them due to the hardening of their hearts. Having lost all sensitivity, they have given themselves over to sensuality so as to indulge in every kind of impurity, with a continual lust for more" (vv. 18–19).

He continues in verses 20–32:

You, however, did not come to know Christ that way. Surely you heard of him and were taught in him in accordance with the truth that is in Jesus. You were taught, with regard to your former way of life, to put off your old self, which is being corrupted by its deceitful desires; to be made new in the attitude of your minds; and to put on the new self, created to be like God in true righteousness and holiness.

Therefore each of you must put off falsehood and speak truthfully to his neighbor, for we are all members of one body. "In your anger do not sin": Do not let the sun go down while you are still angry, and do not give the devil a foothold. He who has been stealing must steal no longer, but must work, doing something useful with his own hands, that he may have something to share with those in need.

Do not let any unwholesome talk come out of your mouths, but only what is helpful for building others up according to their needs, that it may benefit those who listen. And do not grieve the Holy Spirit of God, with whom you were sealed for the day of redemption. Get rid of all bitterness, rage and anger, brawling and slander, along with every form of malice. Be kind and compassionate to one another, forgiving each other, just as in Christ God forgave you.

Putting Off and Putting On

"What is all this 'putting off and putting on'?" you may ask. "How do I do that?"

First you must recognize the actions Paul lists in these verses—put on the new self, put off falsehood, speak truthfully, don't continue in anger, and so on—are not commands, as in, "If you don't do this, God's going to punish you." No, these verses are a list of behaviors that are now possible for you as a child of God. They're consistent with who you are in Christ. They're your new "wardrobe."

At the same time, the negative behaviors Paul mentions—lying, stealing, rage, malice, violence—are incompatible with the new you. They're like old, tattered, dirty clothes that are no longer wanted or needed. They feel uncomfortable and strangely unnatural, because they don't fit anymore. So what do you do? You make the choice to throw them in the trash and begin dressing in a way that more truly expresses your new identity. You put off the old and put on the new.

That choice is not made once and for all. It's made from day to day, circumstance to circumstance. Let's say you are confronted with a familiar but troubling situation. Someone pushes one of your buttons, and you begin to respond the way your old self would have responded. As a new creation in Christ, you can interrupt that response and choose instead to respond according to the values of the new you.

In a situation where the old you would have acted violently, sworn, cursed, stomped, and hit, you now have another option. When those old responses begin, you can choose to put them off: "I don't need to do that anymore." Then you can choose to put on the responses that are more consistent with the new you: gentleness and self-control, for example. Because you are in Christ, you really do have something new to put on! It's in this ongoing way—as circumstances come along that require a choice—that you progressively put off the old and put on the new.

> Becoming more like Christ is an unfolding process; you don't simply graduate one day with a degree in saintliness.

Too often we perceive change in static terms. To really understand this activity of putting off and putting on, though, you need to think of your Christianity in terms of journey rather than arrival. Becoming more like Christ is an unfolding process; you don't simply graduate one day with a degree in saintliness. You don't move in a straight line from point A to point B. Rather, you stagger along toward godliness and Christlikeness on a path that includes ups and downs, roadblocks and curves.

If you think in terms of arrival, you'll always be disappointed with where you are. You'll never be quite who you ought to be or where you ought to be. There is a *process* of new life happening within you. Your prayer needs to be, "Lord, catch me at being old.

Help me to remember that's not me anymore, so I can choose to be the new person I really am."

I'm not talking about behavior modification. This isn't simply a gimmick or a neat idea. *There really is a new you.* In fact, you have been so radically made new that the Scripture calls you "born again." Now the changes in your life that began on the inside are in the process of working their way out, as you make the choice to put off and put on.

All you have to do is make the new-you choice. You don't have to supply the power to carry it out; God does that. The Holy Spirit empowers your choice. You turn the ignition key, and God supplies the engine power. As you make more and more choices God can agree with, join in, and empower, you move ahead in the process of godliness. It is the working of God on the one hand, and it's also you choosing the working of God on the other hand.

A New Attitude

Notice that Ephesians 4:23 says, "Be made new in the attitude of your minds." In aeronautics *attitude* is a technical word. When you fly an airplane, you are always concerned with correct attitude; it has to do with the direction the nose of the plane is going. If you have a down attitude, the nose of the plane is pointing down, and you're in a descent. If the attitude is up, then you're ascending.

That's not far from the meaning of *attitude* in verse 23. Your mind has a lot to do with your mood. If you have a down attitude, then you interpret everything around you—people, circumstances—in a down way. Your attitude takes you down. When you're with other people, you take them down with you.

(Have you ever felt pretty good but noticed three minutes after a certain person enters the room, your mood takes a nosedive? It happens!)

When you became a new creation in Christ, however, a newness began to take hold of your imagination and thought life. The Holy Spirit pointed your attitude up. That new attitude elevates and lifts you; it causes you to have a different perspective and go in a different direction. Now when your thoughts begin to drag you down, you can stop it. It's possible, because you have a new mind. You are able to think in new ways; you aren't stuck in old, destructive thinking habits.

What Are You Telling Yourself?

Self-talk is extremely important. When you do something dumb, for example, what do you tell yourself?

Driving down the road the other day, I was thinking about something dumb I did ten years ago. (The longer you live, the more opportunities you have for stupidity in your life.) I was going along and beating myself half to death about this thing. Then it occurred to me, *What am I doing? Most of the people that were affected by this are dead. It's over and done with and has been for ten years. I handled all of the pieces I needed to; there's no mess left to worry about. It was just a dumb thing, and here I am, ten years later, beating myself up over it!*

Men often describe to me a common bad attitude-habit. On their way to work, they fight with their wives in their imagination. The argument they lost last night, they win on the way to work the next morning. Of course, they never lose these commuter arguments, since they're comprised of all the things they wish they had said.

Have you ever argued with someone in your mind? Do you know that when you do, your brain doesn't distinguish between real and imagined experience? When you rehearse and argue something in your mind, your memory is impacted just as much as if you were physically standing in the same room with the person and arguing aloud. It hurts you, and it hurts your relationship. The next time you see that person, the richness of your relationship is reduced because of the damage you did in your fantasy fight. That's how powerful your mind is!

What can you do? Reject that kind of thinking! Be good to yourself. Be a good parent to yourself. There's a little kid down inside you; keep that child healthy and happy. A healthy child does not commit self-abuse.

When flying a plane, a pilot must constantly check to see which direction the nose of the aircraft is going. As a person being renewed in the attitude of your mind, you need to constantly check the direction your thoughts are taking you (and taking other people). Keep them elevated; keep them pointing up.

Being Angry without Sinning

Ephesians 4:26 talks about another aspect of attitude when it says, "In your anger do not sin." Notice the Bible doesn't teach that the new you cannot or must not get angry. It teaches that when you are angry, you don't have to sin. That means everybody in your life ought to be just as safe with you when you're angry as when you're not. People shouldn't have to change their lives or protect themselves because you're having a bad day. Children especially—they need to know the energy and power generated in you by anger will never ever be vented in a hurtful way toward them. They need to know they're safe with you.

All emotions produce energy. Joy can energize your entire day. Attraction produces energy. Fear produces energy. And anger produces energy—lots of energy. The challenge is determining how you will invest the energy your emotions produce. That's what controlling your emotions means: directing the energy in a positive way.

> **Controlling your emotions means directing the energy in a positive way.**

If you're not able to direct the energy of your anger in nonsinful ways, you're out of control. Nobody else is responsible for your anger, only you! It's a chosen response. It is absolutely inaccurate to claim, "You make me mad." No other person can make you mad. You choose to be angry. Until you take responsibility for that response, you will not be able to put off the attitude of the old you and put on the attitude of the new you.

Because you are a new person in Christ, you have a choice. You can choose to direct your anger in a way that isn't sinful. You can actually use the energy of anger to bring healing, health, and hope.

A good example of this is the creation of Mothers Against Drunk Driving (MADD). The organization was founded by Candy Lightner after her own child was killed by a drunk driver. She was violently angry; who wouldn't be? But she reasoned, "I can spend the rest of my life in bitterness and anger, or I can convert this energy into something positive and work to make sure this kind of tragedy doesn't happen to other families." Because she chose to apply her anger in a positive way, MADD has saved thousands of lives by reducing social tolerance for drunk driving and supporting tough drunk-driving laws.

Confronting the Problem of Anger and Abuse

Unfortunately, uncontrolled anger is a problem among Christian people. If we're going to be honest with ourselves, we must recognize that domestic abuse is a problem in the Christian community. Christians deal with child abuse, verbal abuse, and emotional abuse.

Church leaders are just now coming to realize how deep and how pervasive this problem is, because it's been covered up for so long. I'm not exaggerating when I say hardly a week goes by when at least one of my appointments is not related to an abusive situation. Sometimes almost every appointment is related in some way to a form of abuse—emotional, verbal, or physical; child, parent, or spouse.

I thank God these people are coming for help and that help is available. The good news of Ephesians is that believers are not locked into rage and other deeply ingrained, negative reactions. We have an alternative; a different response is possible. As new people in Christ, we can choose against destructive action and choose instead to be angry without sin.

If you have a problem with your anger, please do two things immediately: (1) take responsibility for it, and (2) get some help. This is crucially important!

Sorry Is Not Enough

Remorse does not solve an anger problem. Let's say a husband assaults his wife in a fit of anger. Afterward he realizes what he did and he feels remorseful. He declares, "I will never do it again." But his anger problem isn't solved. Remorse is a legitimate feeling, because what he did was wrong. But remorse does not guarantee he won't do it again, nor does it heal the pain he caused.

Almost every abused wife comes to a place where she sincerely believes, "His anger is my problem. It's my fault." She comes to accept what her husband has told her over and over again: "If you would just change, I wouldn't have this problem. If you would just do things differently, I wouldn't be angry."

Excuse me! Your anger is never anyone else's problem. Conversely, someone else's anger is never your fault. You have to understand this and take responsibility for your own emotional life. Then, from this responsible posture, you can come to God and say, "I want to put off the old self and put on the new. It's my problem, and I want you to help me with it." It's only when you face the truth that the truth can begin to set you free.

Self-Control in Word and Deed

Being a new person means you are in control of yourself now. You're not just lollygagging around, indulging your appetites and emotions; you're in control. In a godly way, on the basis of your new, godly values, you are investing the energy of your emotions in healthy, constructive ways. You're not using that energy to hurt, destroy, alienate, or tear down. Whereas the old you was out of control, the Holy Spirit has returned self-control to the new you.

Chapter 12: The CHRISTIAN LIFESTYLE

Here is a prayer God will never answer: "Oh God, control my life." God is not interested in controlling your life. He's interested in healing you so powerfully and changing you so deeply that you can be trusted with your own life again. That's the transformation process you can choose now that you are in Christ.

From Taker to Giver

Ephesians 4:28 says, "He who has been stealing must steal no longer, but must work, doing something useful with his own hands, that he may have something to share with those in need." What Paul is talking about here goes beyond taking care of your own basic needs—food, shelter, and the other necessities of life. He says you are to work so you can have something to give to others. It's amazing, isn't it? The new you is not only self-controlled; you're generous! You've been transformed from a taker to a giver. You're motivated to reach out and help other people who are in need. Generosity never leads to stealing or defrauding; it only motivates us to work and to give.

From Destroyer to Builder

Paul continues in verse 29, "Do not let any unwholesome talk come out of your mouths, but only what is helpful for building others up according to their needs, that it may benefit those who listen." Paul is talking here about verbal abuse. Whenever someone else's comments or conversation makes you feel bad about yourself or less as a person, you're being verbally abused. That's "unwholesome talk"—speech that tears down and causes people to think less of themselves. Tearing people down verbally attacks their sense of value and worth. They walk away thinking they really are bad, ugly, hopeless, or worthless.

Instead of tearing down, Paul says, you are to speak "only what is helpful for building others up." That means encouraging people with your words. Constructive talk is the opposite of verbal abuse. It is sensitive and designed to meet other people's needs. It benefits those who listen. They walk away stronger and better for having had a conversation with you.

Do you talk in a way that is beneficial to the people who listen? I often meet people who practice this kind of constructive speech. As they talk, I feel as if I'm standing up straighter on the inside, just growing taller and feeling good. When they walk away, I think, *I'm really glad I met them today.* The conversation may have taken thirty seconds; it may have taken fifteen minutes; it may have happened over lunch; it may have happened in a chance meeting at the mall—but somehow when they walked away, I felt warmed by the encounter.

I'm reminded of an eighty-six-year-old woman I know whose visits are always hard on me. All the events of her life are keyed around various sicknesses. If you bring up a certain date, she'll say, "I remember, that was the year my son had pneumonia." If you mention something that happened in 1956, she'll say, "Yes, that's the year my husband had a terrible attack of asthma. We just about lost him." We've heard about her husband's attack of asthma for twenty years now—1956, the year of asthma; 1968, the year of pneumonia. I walk away saying, "Oh, boy." I have to recover from the conversations!

My wife's father is ninety years old, but he's just the opposite of this woman. He's a strong Norwegian named Ole Paulson. For forty-two years he ran Ole's Texaco in the small town of

Chapter 12: The CHRISTIAN LIFESTYLE

Woodburn, south of Portland, Oregon. Plenty of social conversation and town business took place at Ole's. If you wanted to know how Mrs. Brown's surgery went yesterday, you would find out faster at Ole's than by calling the hospital. I spent a lot of time at that Texaco station when I was dating Barbara; it was a fun, good-natured, happy place.

I called Ole the other day and asked, "Ole, how are you doing?"

"Well," he said, "I shot a 78 on the golf course today!"

He shot 78! "Well," I said, "that's great. That's below your age!"

Ole has had his share of sicknesses, and his family has had its share of sorrows; but when you talk to him, he remembers the years as being full of positive things. You walk away from a conversation with Ole feeling that life is OK, life is good. That's talk that benefits, that builds up. That's how the new you is meant to talk.

A Polaroid Snapshot

Paul ends Ephesians 4 this way: "And do not grieve the Holy Spirit of God, with whom you were sealed for the day of redemption. Get rid of all bitterness, rage and anger, brawling and slander, along with every form of malice. Be kind and compassionate to one another, forgiving each other, just as in Christ God forgave you" (vv. 30–32).

This is who you *really* are: a self-controlled person who doesn't lie but speaks truthfully; who is no longer greedy and selfish, but giving; who chooses joy and love over bitterness. You no longer have to rage out of control with anger; you no longer have to be involved in slander or other hurtful or malicious activities. You are able to talk in ways that benefit others—not selfishly reacting, but lovingly responding into other people's lives. That's who you really are. That's you. That's a Polaroid snapshot.

You're not someone who is learning a loving technique; you're a loving person. You're not someone who is learning a formula for controlling anger; you're a person who is self-controlled. You're not someone repeating nice words to win Brownie points from your audience; you're a sensitive, constructive speaker.

Understand, when we talk about ministry, we're talking not about what you do; we're talking about who you are. You don't *have* a ministry; you *are* a ministry. That's a very important distinction. Ministry is always expressed in terms of being. You can do ministering things and not minister. In Ephesians 4 Paul is not giving you things to do; he's showing you who you are. And if you're in the process of becoming the person he describes, you can't help but minister.

Ole ministers to me, but certainly not by preaching me sermons. I told him once, "Dad, you ought to write a book on how to retire and stay happy." Because he's done that so well, I watch him and listen to him. He ministers to me with his life, by being who he is.

Honor the Nudge

Be the person you really are. *Choose into* your true identity. When you catch yourself going another way, know that you have an option. The Holy Spirit is at work inside you. Don't you feel a little nudge sometimes, when you're reacting in the old-you way; and you know if you'd just stop for a second—one second of sanity—the Holy Spirit would give you the right new-you response? How often do you ignore the nudge and blow on through, then find yourself asking for forgiveness and trying to repair the damage later?

170

Chapter 12: The CHRISTIAN LIFESTYLE

Just take a moment for sanity. Take a moment for the new you. Step back. Honor that little nudge—it's the Holy Spirit prompting you. If you honor the nudge and make the right choice according to who you are in Christ, he'll empower that choice. And you'll find you like the person you're becoming.

Sometimes I look in the mirror and say to that person looking back at me, "You know, Jesus is doing a really good job on you. You're better than I ever thought you'd be." That's not pride; that's truth. I mean, considering what he had to work with, he's doing all right! He's doing far better than I ever could have done on my own.

Embrace God's work in you. Choose into it. Sometimes you may choose with an "ouch!" That's OK; maybe something needed to be chipped off so the image of Christ could be seen more clearly in you.

Choose to put on your new identity. It's your choice; Jesus Christ will never make the choice for you. I see a lot of people sitting around waiting for Jesus to change them. If you do that, you'll be waiting a long time. Why? Because you've already been changed. What you have to do now is choose into the change.

There are many choruses and songs that beg Jesus to change us. Don't waste your breath. You're either a new creature or you're not. You can't be half in and half out. You're either born again or you're not. What does the Scripture say? It says that you're a new creature in Christ Jesus. That's a fact. How much more change do you want?

So go ahead, choose into your new identity. Turn the ignition key. After all, God is able to do "immeasurably more than all we ask or imagine, according to his power that is at work within us" (Ephesians 3:20). He will empower you to live out your choice.

Chapter 13

A LIFE of LOVE

Ed Janes has been part of our congregation for a dozen years or so. He's forty-eight, the father of three, and works as a mail carrier. Some time ago he was featured in our Sunday paper, in the following front-page story titled, "Faith Motivates Kenmore Man to Donate Organ":

Ed Janes and Ryan Yong grew up on opposite sides of the world. They don't believe in the same God. They eat different foods and speak different languages. In the seven years they have worked together at the Midlakes Post Office in Bellevue, Janes and Yong have never had a conversation about anything personal. They are only coworkers. But recently, they learned they are more alike on the inside than even family.

When Ryan learned he had kidney failure, all avenues for a transplant were explored to no avail. His long absence from work caused his desperate condition to become known by his coworkers. Yong tells how when he returned to work, Ed came up to him and said simply, "Test me." What Ryan thought was a joke at first proved to be an offer of pure love.

It was a good match, and Janes and Yong were rolled into adjacent operating rooms where, during seven hours of intensive surgery, doctors removed a kidney from Janes and transplanted it into Yong. When asked why he would do such a thing, Ed responds, "Why wouldn't you do that? It shouldn't be amazing. Everyone should treat each other like a brother."

He drew on his faith in God to offer his kidney. He believes Jesus would have done the same.

Ryan Yong sums it up beautifully, "He has given me new life."

Imitators of God

Ephesians 5:1 begins with this amazing statement: "Be imitators of God, therefore, as dearly loved children and live a life of love, just as Christ loved us and gave himself up for us as a fragrant offering and sacrifice to God."

"Be imitators of God." What does that phrase mean? How can we, as mere mortals, imitate the Creator of heaven and earth? Well, whatever else that phrase means, it carries this implication: Give God visibility in your world. Make him be seen. Allow him to be known through you. That's what you do when you imitate someone. That's what Ed Janes did.

"Be imitators of God." Live out the nature of God in your world, so the people around you can eventually come to the conclusion that God is a God of love. Most people have never given a good God much thought. Yet that's exactly the kind of God Jesus came to reveal. You and I need to live in such a way that people can draw the bottom-line conclusion, "You know, to watch you and be around you, I am not only starting to believe in God, I'm starting to believe in a God who loves me. Maybe he's not mad at me after all; maybe he's not out to get me. Maybe he's not the source of evil. The way you talk and act makes me wonder. *Could you tell me about this God?*"

Dearly Loved

Notice that the verse says we imitate God as "dearly loved children." Do you know you are now, at this very moment, a dearly loved child of God? Hopefully by this point in the book, you have come to accept that truth. You can only imitate a loving God if you are experiencing a loving God.

"Well, what about the rotten day I had last week? What about that time I lost my temper with my spouse? What did God think of me that day?"

He loved you. He never stops loving you.

Of course, I can tell you over and over again that God loves you. But my telling you will never get the job done. Something has to happen inside you spiritually so you can begin to consistently hear the voice of the Father saying, "You're my child. I love you, and I'm pleased with you."

One of the things that's important to me as a parent is to convey to my children what I think of them, how they look in my eyes. Nobody sees them the way I do. Other people can have opinions, but I want them to know what Dad sees—how proud I am of who they are and who they are becoming.

Sadly, many kids never know what their parents see. Or they

do know—and what Mom or Dad communicates to them is damaging and destructive. Children tend to become what they sense their parents see them to be.

My goal is to have a solid adult friendship with my kids. But I will always be their dad. When I visit my grown children, I can tell they're still looking to see, "What does Dad think of me?" One daughter who is in her thirties made a very destructive decision a little while back. It scared her and all of us. I was at a conference in Montana and was about to fly to California. When I heard what was going on, I changed my flight plan and arranged a horrible connection so I could make a five-hour stopover in the city where she lives. I called and invited her to come meet me at the airport.

"Hon, why didn't you just give me a call?" I asked. "I wouldn't try to tell you what to do. I would just be a sounding board. I love you."

"I didn't call because I figured you'd think I was a bad person," she said.

I proceeded to explain to her that good people make bad decisions all the time. Just because you make a bad decision doesn't make you a bad person! I certainly didn't love her any less. She needed to hear that, not from just anybody, but from Dad.

The Basis for Ministry

I sincerely hope you can hear your heavenly Father saying to you, even when you make a bad decision, "You're my child. I love you!" Until you understand and embrace the fact that God loves you unconditionally, you will never be able to live a life of true, God-imitating love. You will simply work God and work other people in a foolish attempt to grab the love you want. Selfishly, you will try to love yourself through others. You will manipulate your relationships to satisfy your sagging ego and get your love needs met. You will be totally incapable of pure ministry.

If I were preaching with the express purpose of being loved by my listeners, I could not minister to them. Now, I don't want to be hated, but neither is it my goal to be loved (or even liked) by those I minister to. I can live without that. I don't mean to sound obnoxious, arbitrary, or prideful; that's not the way I feel. But my life does not depend on your opinion of me. I can handle whatever you think. Why? Because I know God loves me. I know he's my Father, and I know I love him.

When I go to speak to a new group—let's say it's your group—I don't have to work to get you to like me. I can simply minister to you in the love of the Father. If my focus is to get you to like me, then I'll do everything I can to be liked by you, and I'll go home feeling liked. You'll go home thinking, *Why did I waste my time on that?*

> To the degree you and I can rest in the security of God's love, we can minister his love to others.

To the degree you and I can rest in the security of God's love, we can minister his love to others. As we embrace the love of God for us, we can then turn around and imitate what we know. We can live a life of love.

In Ephesians 5 Paul gives us a list of seven keys for living such a life. Together they are a description of the loving lifestyle God intends for his covenant people. When I say, "I love you," this is what I'm talking about. I'm not talking about the emotional, fuzzy, syrupy, gushy stuff we typically call love; I'm talking about following through with the actions on this list.

1. Live Purely

Ephesians 5:3–4 says, "But among you there must not be even a hint of sexual immorality, or of any kind of impurity, or of greed, because these are improper for God's holy people. Nor should there be obscenity, foolish talk or coarse joking, which are out of place, but rather thanksgiving."

When you choose to live a pure life, you are loving God, your brothers and sisters in Christ, and other people. Every time you face a temptation of impurity and make the choice for purity, you are committing an act of love. Why? Because you are keeping your heart and mind clean and clear, so God's love can flow through you unhindered. You're not burdened by guilt, regret, or the consequences of sin. You are able to minister freely.

2. Live as Light in the Darkness

Paul writes in verses 8–14:

> For you were once darkness, but now you are light in the Lord. Live as children of light (for the fruit of the light consists in all goodness, righteousness and truth) and find out what pleases the Lord. Having nothing to do with the fruitless deeds of darkness, but rather expose them. For it is shameful even to mention what the disobedient do in secret. But everything exposed by the light becomes visible, for it is light that makes everything visible. This is why it is said:
>
> "Wake up, O sleeper,

rise from the dead,

and Christ will shine on you."

What does light look like? According to Paul, it looks like goodness, righteousness, and truth. These are the ingredients of light. So wherever you are in this immoral, impure, and greedy world, you, as a child of light, bring goodness and righteousness and truth by your very presence. That's what light brings to a dark place.

Light is dominant. You control darkness with light; you don't control light with darkness. When you are living as light, you are lighting the darkness for others. You are living a life of love.

3. Live Wisely and Alert to Opportunity

Verses 15–17 continue, "Be very careful, then, how you live—not as unwise but as wise, making the most of every opportunity, because the days are evil. Therefore do not be foolish, but understand what the Lord's will is."

Evil days offer unique opportunities for ministry. That's because evil days result in brokenness and pain. They cause people to question even their most basic beliefs. Remember what I wrote earlier? Evil is l-i-v-e spelled backward. Evil days are those days that crash around people's heads and threaten the very fiber of their lives.

As Christians we're not here to campaign against evil days. We're not here to be issue-mongers and yell and scream about the darkness. It bothers me (worse than that, but that's the word I'll use) when Christians align themselves politically and fight. (My chances of being misunderstood here are huge, but I'll risk it.) We are not here to ensure that nothing evil or bad ever takes place. We live on a planet where evil exists. In fact, the Scripture says that in the last days evil will increase. The world will fall apart.

And that's OK! Evil days are what we're about. It's in the dark days that we, as people of light, can really make a difference. Not because we have placards or votes or political clout, but because we have *God in us*. Remember the huge principle we developed in chapter 1: "Christ in you is the hope of glory."

You're here for a purpose. Be alert, be awake. Don't live in a way that focuses on getting everything you want. Instead, be wise and take advantage of every opportunity you have to minister to others in the name of Jesus.

> You're safe in the middle of the most evil of evil days because the Spirit of Christ lives in you.

"But," you say, "the days are *really* bad."

Exactly! But they're not bad for you. You're safe in the middle of the most evil of evil days because the Spirit of Christ lives in you. The evil won't touch you. That's not to say you won't get hurt; it just means evil won't be lethal at your address. It can't kill you. Why not? Because Jesus has destroyed the power of death. Death is no longer a threat to the covenant people of God.

So don't waste your breath cursing evil. Instead, go about the business of being the light of God in a dark place. Bring Jesus Christ into the lives of those people who are being crushed and hurt and damaged and destroyed. Every time you respond in Jesus's name to the pain and hurt of another person, every time you're alert to a person's need and act into that need in the name of Jesus, you commit an act of love—not just to that person, but to me, to your brothers and sisters in Christ, to Jesus.

4. Live Spiritually

Ephesians 5:18 says, "Do not get drunk on wine, which leads to debauchery. Instead, be filled with the Spirit."

Every time you give place to the indwelling and infilling of the Holy Spirit, you are committing an act of love. Being filled with the Spirit is choosing the right intoxicant—the right source of joy and peace. Unlike other intoxicants, the Holy Spirit makes you sharp and alert, not dull and confused. Your perception of reality is increased, not decreased. You are enabled to live purely and wisely; you're fully prepared to respond to the needs of others in a godly and loving way.

You are going to be filled with something, right? Choose the Holy Spirit. It's an act of love.

5. Live in Fellowship

Fellowship can be described as the people of God enjoying one another and enjoying God together. Verse 19 gives us a picture of this: "Speak to one another with psalms, hymns and spiritual songs. Sing and make music in your heart to the Lord." That's what it was like last Sunday at our church. We were worshiping the Lord and singing and sharing together. Everything we did was an act of love.

Throughout this book I've stressed that Monday is an important day. And it is. But the demands of Monday are the reason it's so vital for believers to come together on Sunday. We need the

181

encouragement we get from one another. We need the support, the understanding. We need the love. These are things we don't get from the world; we only get them from each other.

You're living a life of love when you allow yourself to be a part of a group of believers. You're living a life of love when you become an active contributor, an active giver to your brothers and sisters in Christ. Fellowship is not watching while other people sing; it demands participation. *You* sing, *you* talk, *you* share. You don't simply observe. You're not in fellowship because you're present; you're in fellowship because you're participating. And that's an act of love.

Anytime you make the decision to be in fellowship with others who share your covenant relationship with God—in the corporate assembly of the church; in smaller meetings; in Bible studies; in any gathering of believers—that's an act of love. You're loving the individuals who are meeting with you. You're loving me. You're loving the body of Christ. Gathering with other believers is an act of love in the eyes of our Father.

6. Live Gratefully

Verse 20 continues, "Always giving thanks to God the Father for everything, in the name of our Lord Jesus Christ." Whenever you don't complain and bellyache but choose instead to be grateful— for your marriage, your children, your home, your health, your job—that's an act of love. Gratefulness is a sign that you know God; you understand he is the source of everything good in your life. When other people see that you know God this way, they can't help but be drawn to you. If you're constantly grumbling, however, your opportunities for ministry disintegrate. Who wants to be around a chronic complainer? That's why, when you choose to be grateful, you're living a life of love.

7. Live Submissively

Verse 21 says, "Submit to one another out of reverence for Christ." I can't think of many words that have been maligned as much as this one word, *submit*. The idea of submission has been applied to everything from a Tarzan/Jane model for marriage to blind obedience to despotic church rulers.

Yet the word has nothing to do with authority—not in this passage or in the normal way it's used in Scripture in general. Submission doesn't imply that someone has authority over you. If it did, how could we all be in submission to one another, as this verse demands? How can everybody have authority over everybody? That makes no sense.

Submission doesn't mean we align ourselves hierarchically. Over the last thirty years, we have seen the tragic misuse of so-called submission teaching in the horrific news stories about Jim Jones in Guyana and David Koresh in Waco, Texas. Those are examples of wrong teaching taken to a fatal extreme. Other abuses—less lethal, but still destructive—continue in many churches and ministries today, even though manipulative leadership is not and never has been a part of the Bible's concept of submission.

The word *submit* actually means to be soft, to give in. (Like my stomach—it used to be less submissive, but now you can push it; it's soft, and it gives in.) Submitted people are not rigid, abrasive, brittle, or hard. They're open; they can be influenced. When I practice submission, I show that I value you. When you speak, I listen, I hear; I let what you're saying to me penetrate my head and my heart. It's a matter of my attitude toward you. An attitude of submission means I'll receive you as a person, not as a class or category. Whether you're of high degree or low degree; whatever your color, age, race, or gender; I'll receive you and value you.

That's what Paul means when he says, "Submit to one another." Value one another; listen to one another. Don't patronize or look down on one another. Stand eye to eye and see each other as respected brothers and sisters in the same family of God.

Husbands, Wives, and the S-Word

Springboarding from this basic understanding, Paul continues: "Wives, submit to your husbands as to the Lord. For the husband is the head of the wife as Christ is the head of the church, his body, of which he is the Savior. Now as the church submits to Christ, so also wives should submit to their husbands in everything" (vv. 22–24).

From these verses through the first half of Ephesians chapter 6, Paul proceeds to apply the concept of submission to three important life circumstances: living submissively in your marriage; living submissively in your family (see Ephesians 6:1–4); and living submissively in your workplace (see Ephesians 6:5–9). Since the first of these three is often the most controversial, we'll look at it more closely.

Understand, submission in marriage is mutual. It's reciprocal. Both partners are meant to value and appreciate one another. I've heard husbands insist, "The Bible says my wife has to submit to me. It doesn't say I have to submit to my wife." Of course it does, in Ephesians 5:21. We already discussed it: "Submit to one another out of reverence for Christ." You're either a "one" or an "another." There's no third alternative.

Where would a husband get such a misguided idea? Perhaps it can be traced to a common mistranslation of the passage in Genesis where Eve is called Adam's "helpmeet," a term that implies an inferior position. The fact is, the Hebrew language doesn't have a word that can be translated "helpmeet." The actual, literal translation is "a helper meet for him"—that is, "a helper that meets him." This is someone on par with him, who meets him at his level. Someone into whose eyes he can stand and look directly. Someone whose eyes answer back with intelligence and knowing. Someone in whom he sees something that is like himself.

Think about it: what was Adam doing just before God gave him a divine anesthetic and took the extra rib he'd put there (it wasn't an afterthought) to form the woman? Adam had been naming the animals. In Hebrew, naming carries the idea of "coming to know." Adam was coming to fully know and understand the animal kingdom so that he could identify each animal's characteristics and call it by its true nature. But in that process he did not find a partner, an equal, someone he could see himself in.

So he gets the anesthetic, the rib is gone, the woman is there, and bingo—he wakes up.

Have you ever been under anesthesia? Isn't it interesting that you lose no time? I was put under one time for a medical procedure, and when I woke up, I asked, "When are you going to start?" They answered, "We've been done for four hours."

Now I wasn't there, so I don't know; but just *suppose* it was that way for Adam. The last thing he sees is a monkey, and then he wakes up and there's Eve, and he says, "Whoa!" He recognizes, "This is now bone of my bones and flesh of my flesh" (Genesis 2:23). Unlike any of the creatures he's just named and over which he's been given dominion, Eve is the helper who can stand and meet him eye to eye, who can see and understand him in his human person and nature. She is someone who shares the unique qualities of his humanity, someone with whom submission can be mutual.

You've Got to Be Kidding!

Paul continues in verses 25–33:

> Husbands, love your wives, just as Christ loved the church and gave himself up for her to make her holy, cleansing her by the washing with water through the word, and to present her to himself as a radiant church, without stain or wrinkle or any other blemish, but holy and blameless. In this same way, husbands ought to love their wives as their own bodies. He who loves his wife loves himself. After all, no one ever hated his own body, but he feeds and cares for it, just as Christ does the church—for we are members of his body. "For this reason a man will leave his father and mother and be united to his wife, and the two will become one flesh." This is a profound mystery—but I am talking about Christ and the church. However, each one of you also must love his wife as he loves himself, and the wife must respect her husband.

Believe it or not, these were preposterous words. "Husbands, love your wives" doesn't sound strange to us, living more than nineteen centuries after the words were written. But it definitely sounded strange to the people back in Paul's day. You see, in the Greek-Gentile world of the first century, it never dawned on husbands to love their wives. You didn't do that with wives.

Wives were for the sole purpose of giving men legitimate children and caring for their homes and belongings. Love was reserved for an elite group of women known as the hetaerae. The hetaerae were specially educated to be companions, intellectually and sexually, to men in the Greek upper class. They were the official mistresses—the high-class prostitutes.

You didn't love your wife; why would you? She didn't know anything except how to have kids and take care of the house. You married her, sure, because you needed someone to do those things; but then you went and loved the woman you were intended to love, one of the hetaerae. That was the thinking of upper-class Ephesian husbands. It sounds strange to us, but it was their world.

So when Paul wrote to these Christian men, "Husbands, love your wives," they probably reacted: "What are you talking about? You've got to be kidding!" When he explained the way Jesus loves the church—like a bride—he was explaining a concept that was totally foreign to them. But what an important concept! He wanted these Ephesian believers to understand the way Jesus loves the church and the way Jesus loved them was the way they were supposed to love their wives.

Paul didn't just shock the men. When he wrote that "the wife must respect her husband" (v. 33), the wives must have thought, *Are you kidding? Why would any wife do that?* In another place in Scripture, the Greek word *phileo* is used, meaning that a wife is to be "a friend" to her husband. Wives in Ephesus in those days weren't their husbands' friends; the hetaerae were the friends. The wives had the household slaves and other women to be friends with.

So in both cases, speaking to husbands and to wives, Paul used this passage in Ephesians 5 to define a marriage relationship that was foreign to them—a relationship of mutual appreciation, respect, and submission. The first-century Ephesians didn't understand it. And I have to admit, I'm concerned that if our modern culture keeps going the way it is, one day we'll have that same strange look when we read, "Husbands, love your wives. Wives, respect your husbands."

"Really?" we'll say.

May it never be!

As Christians we need to be sure we're applying the principle of submission in our husband-and-wife relationships; and not only there, but also in our parent-child relationships and employer-employee relationships. (Read Ephesians 6:1–9 to see what Paul had to say about these latter two.) You see, whenever we take the posture of submitting to one another—in our marriages, in our homes, in our workplaces—we're living a life of love. Every time you respond in submission to the people in your life, you're committing an act of love.

Are you living the life of love God intends for you? Go back over the seven keys in this chapter and see where you are loving and where you are not. Whenever you make the choice to love in one of these ways, you show the people around you that God is a good God. And you open the floodgates for God to love them—through you.

NOT in My NEIGHBORHOOD!

What if our strategic placement in the world was not just for the purpose of expressing the life of Christ, but also designed to block the inroads of evil at key places in the culture?

Remarkably, it is true. God has taken his relocation—his living in us—to a radical extreme. He has chosen not to give us techniques. He hasn't commanded us to develop monolithic institutions to combat evil. He has chosen not to engage the enemy economically or even politically. Rather, he has chosen to define the crucial points where evil threatens, where Satan's strategies seem most likely to succeed, and put a Spirit-filled believer there. Like pieces on a chessboard or the positioning of missiles and troops in war, Christians are strategically and intentionally placed to neutralize the enemy's effectiveness and frustrate his plans.

This strategy is not designed to defeat human beings—flesh and blood. God never views individual people as enemies. They may see *him* as their enemy, but he never looks at them that way. No, this strategy engages an entirely different level of reality described in Ephesians 6:12 as the realm of spiritual "rulers," "authorities," "powers," and "forces of evil."

Because God knows we're in a spiritual fight, he has created special armor for us to wear—armor designed to frustrate the purposes and plans of the spiritual forces of evil. Paul tells us in Ephesians 6:11–12, "Put on the full armor of God so that you can take your stand against the devil's schemes. For our struggle is not against flesh and blood, but against the rulers, against the authorities, against the powers of this dark world and against the spiritual forces of evil in the heavenly realms."

> If you have on the full armor of God, when everyone and everything else has fallen down, you will still be standing.

Why should you, as a covenant believer, put on this armor? For two specific reasons: First, so you can "take your stand against the devil's schemes"—that is, so his plans won't work where you are. Not only will they not work against you, they won't work in the place where God has strategically positioned you.

The second reason is found in verse 13: "Therefore put on the full armor of God, so that when the day of evil comes, you may be able to stand your ground, and after you have done everything, to stand." In other words, when evil comes in, it will hit you and go no further. The tsunami of evil stops with you! Being strong and covered in the full armor of God is not just for your own protection; it's so you can take your position as a frustration and a roadblock to the schemes of Satan and the inroads of evil.

Understand, that means Christ may very well station you at the dark places where evil is making the greatest assault. He will place you there strategically, intentionally, so evil will go no further. It won't be comfortable, because the evil will come and crash against you; but it will not get past you.

Standing Your Ground

If you have on the full armor of God, when everyone and everything else has fallen down, you will still be standing. Evil will heap up against you, but it will go no further, because you're a person who has these qualities in your life: "Stand firm then, with the belt of truth buckled around your waist, with the breastplate of righteousness in place, and with your feet fitted with the readiness that comes from the gospel of peace. In addition to all this, take up the shield of faith, with which you can extinguish all the flaming arrows of the evil one. Take the helmet of salvation and the sword of the Spirit, which is the word of God" (vv. 14–17).

Truth, righteousness, peace, faith, salvation (wholeness), and the Word of God: these are the qualities and commodities that frustrate the purposes of Satan. To the degree that you are a person of truth; a person in whom righteousness dwells, who is committed to what's right; a person whose life is dedicated to peace (not peace at any cost, but the peace that's born of God); a person of faith; a person living in the wholeness of salvation; a person who not only knows the Word of God, but also walks it out—to that degree, you are someone who is blocking the strategies of Satan. To the degree you participate in the opposite of these, you are helping promote the strategies of Satan; you are a gateway for evil.

The Belt of Truth

The first piece of armor Paul mentions in Ephesians 6:14 is the "belt of truth." Why is truth so important? Truth frustrates Satan, because his kingdom is based entirely upon deception and lies. Since the cross, Satan has had no legitimate power base. Scripture tells us that Jesus destroyed the works of the enemy (see 1 John 3:8). Christ's death on the cross destroyed the base from which Satan worked; it destroyed his inherent power.

The only power Satan has now is the power of lies. Of course, the power of a lie is a very great power if, in fact, we can be convinced the lie is true. When we believe a lie to be true, it becomes our reality. If I'm lying to you and you're buying it, I'm gaining power over you. But if your wife happens to know the truth, and she leans over and whispers the truth to you, suddenly the power of my lie is broken. That's it; it's over.

As soon as you know the truth, the truth will set you free. Free from what? Free from the power of the lie. And as a Spirit-filled, covenant believer, the truth is always available to you. Jesus promised, "The Spirit of truth . . . will guide you into all truth" (John 16:13).

If, on the other hand, you participate in denial, untruth, and exaggerated reality, you empower Satan in your life. If you believe his lies about you, about God, about the world, about your marriage, your friends, your kids, you give him a power base right where you are.

Facing Reality

A mother of three was weeping in my office, concerned she was losing her marriage of twelve years. She told me that she and her husband were not communicating; they were constantly arguing and fighting instead. He was working extremely long hours, and he was always tired. She was confused and afraid.

I sent her out of the room and called the husband in. "How's your marriage?" I asked.

"Never been better. Doing fine. I'm working long hours, but that will pass. We're just great. Why do you ask?"

So I asked the wife to return. "Have the two of you met?" I inquired. "Each of you have just described entirely different marriages."

I've pastored long enough to know the marriage was probably not as bad as the wife thought nor as good as the husband thought. (We men have a strange ability to idealize a perfect marriage and pretend it's ours, against all reality.) Is there hope for such a marriage? Yes, if both partners face the truth. But unless they face reality, they will lose something extremely precious.

Things are not the way you *hope* they are; they are the way they are. Satan doesn't want you to face that; he doesn't want you to face the truth and take responsibility. He wants you to always make your problems somebody else's; that way they will never be solved.

"If Mom and Dad had just raised me differently, I wouldn't be such a troubled person. It's really not my fault." As long as you hold that view, you'll never be free.

"If my wife would just change, I wouldn't have this problem." Excuse me? You're the problem, not your wife. If you had married someone else, you'd still have the problem. If you had married *nobody*, you'd still have the problem. *You're* the problem.

All of us need to stand tall, look in the mirror, and say, "You're the problem." (I'm reminded of a bumper sticker I once saw that read, "Objects in the mirror are dumber than they appear.") Once we face the truth, the truth will set us free.

The Seat of Life

Notice verse 14 says that the belt of truth is "buckled around your waist." In ancient times, the waist and lower abdomen were considered the seat of life. In a similar way, truth is the "seat of life" for believers. It is central to who we are. Our very lives depend upon the truth of God and his Word.

The waist is also a balance point. If you're in a battle, you don't watch the opponent's eyes or arms only; you try to watch his waist. A person can move everything else, but where his tummy points is where he's really going to go. Even when you play basketball, you watch your opponent's belly button, because where it goes, he goes. You can't be fooled if you watch his waist. In this sense, then, wearing the belt of truth means keeping truth at your center.

Unfortunately, we can be very convincing liars—so convincing that we can even lie to ourselves. My grandma used to say, "If you tell a lie long enough, you'll start believing it yourself." I don't know how she knew that, but she was right.

It's painful to admit, but I've noticed that many Christians lie. In fact, the biggest lies I've been told haven't come from the unbelievers in my life, but from believers. Christians lie about their successes. They give their word and don't keep it. They sign a contract and then don't pay. They lie on their tax returns. When their kids get into trouble at school, they lie about their kids. I don't get it. I'm not indicting anyone; I just don't understand why we—why I—have such a capacity to lie.

Chapter 14: NOT in My NEIGHBORHOOD!

Lying is habit-forming. Over time it will cause you to exaggerate when you don't need to; to deny when there's no purpose; to lie, even when the truth would be more to your advantage. Unfortunately, to the degree you allow untruthfulness to become a regular part of your life, to that degree you empower Satan in all areas of your life—you become someone through whom evil can easily pass.

A Culture of Deception

We live in a world that has given away its absolutes. Truth is no longer important; only expediency matters. People often do and say whatever they have to in order to get what they want. We know this and we look the other way. A high percentage of the advertisements on television are not truthful. But that's OK; we know the ads aren't true, so it's all right. No big deal.

We live in a world that is steeped in deception. That's why it's so important for you and me, as covenant people of God, to have truth at the very center of our being. If we don't, deceptiveness will seep in and permeate everything. We have been strategically placed to be those points in our culture where lies and deception can't seep through. No matter how much of the world's deception heaps up against us, it shouldn't be able to get past us. The fact that so much *has* gotten past us is the reason our society is in the mess it's in.

In the last two decades I've been appalled to see the kind of Christianity that has been advertised to a fallen world. Scandals involving Christian leaders have been paraded across front pages and TV screens by a voracious media. People have been deeply hurt, even destroyed. The tragedy is not that the media has had a circus; it's that there has been so much to report. The stories have been true! The very places where evil should have been blocked have instead provided avenues for its venom to enter and kill.

You and I need to buckle our belts! Our prayer needs to be, *Jesus, make us people in whom truth dwells at the very core of our being—people who are centered in truth.*

The Breastplate of Righteousness

Next, Paul encourages us to put "the breastplate of righteousness in place." A soldier's breastplate covers his heart. And that's what righteousness has to do with: your heart. If you are righteous in your heart, you have a commitment to do what's right. You may do something wrong from time to time; but because you have a right heart, you realize what you've done, straighten it out, and get on with life. It's not that you never sin. It's that when you sin, you know it and you repent.

The contrast between a right heart and a wrong heart is illustrated in the lives of Saul and David. Saul looked good but wasn't. David didn't look so good but was. Saul looked like a king, but he didn't have the heart of a king. Not once in Saul's career did he take responsibility for any wrong he did—even when he was caught red-handed by the prophet Samuel.

One time Samuel asked, "Did you sacrifice the cows like you were supposed to?"

Saul answered, "I sure did."

"Then whose cows are those mooing over here?"

(This is a free translation. See 1 Samuel 15:12–29 for the whole story.)

"Well, I just kept some of the better ones. The people talked me into it."

"You sinned," Samuel accused.

"I sinned," admitted Saul.

But Saul used a different Hebrew word for *sin* than Samuel did. The word Saul used meant, "I made a little mistake." So Samuel announced, "Today this kingdom is taken away from you, because you don't have the heart of a king. You didn't make a little mistake, Saul. You sinned!"

David's response to sin was far different from Saul's. You know the story. David had an affair with a married woman named Bathsheba. Afterward, he had her husband killed. You can read all about it in 2 Samuel 11–12. It's shocking! But here's the difference between David and Saul: when the prophet Nathan pointed out his sin, David confessed, "I have sinned before God and man." The word he used didn't mean, "I made a little mistake." No, David used the deepest, most profound Hebrew word he could find for his sinful actions: "I have grossly failed both God and man." Then he fell on his face in repentance.

David had a righteous heart. It wasn't that he didn't sin; it was that when he was confronted with the conviction of the Holy Spirit, he owned up to his sin. "Oh God, forgive me." That's a righteous heart. It doesn't try to deflect responsibility and blame other people. Saul is the perfect example of someone who blamed other people for his problems. David is a perfect example of someone who never did.

The Readiness of Peace

Paul names the next piece of spiritual armor in Ephesians 6:15: "And with your feet fitted with the readiness that comes from the gospel of peace." The word *readiness* here is interesting. It's translated in some places as "preparation" and has to do with what you're standing on. You're ready because of the foundation you're on. If you're standing on solid ground—as opposed to a slippery slope—you're in a posture of strength; and because of that posture you're ready to move.

Imagine yourself standing several inches deep in thick, gooey mud. Try to jump. You don't get very far, do you? Your feet are stuck; they hold you down. Now imagine yourself standing on a firm foundation—a cement pavement, let's say—and making that same jump. This time you go up, right? That's the picture here in verse 15. When you're standing on the firm foundation of the gospel of peace, you are ready to jump. You are ready to move.

> As covenant people we "wear" the good news of peace.

As covenant people we "wear" the good news of peace. We are people of peace, not violence. "Blessed are the peacemakers," Jesus said (Matthew 5:9). We resolve conflict, not cause it. When you come into an angry, divisive place, the result of your presence ought to be more peace, not more discord. Whether it's a church fight, a neighborhood fight, a political fight, a social fight, whatever the fight—you don't jump in and add fuel to the fire. Adding fuel to the fire puts you in a precarious, slippery position, making it impossible for you to act or move as Christ would have you do. Because your feet aren't planted firmly in the gospel of peace, Satan can take you down, along with everyone else. Evil will overrun your position.

If your feet are planted on peace, however, Satan's schemes

cannot operate in your life. You may be living in a world full of discord, but you're not participating in the violence and anxiety and corruption that's all around you. You're not mad at anyone, not looking for a fight, not trying to get even, not trying to make sure other people get what's coming to them. You have staked a position beyond which evil cannot go. When Satan's fury and conflict and anger come against you, you stand. You stand in your home, in your workplace, and in your culture. You are grounded in the peace of God.

The Shield of Faith

According to Paul, all of Satan's attack weapons can be extinguished with one item: faith. Ephesians 6:16 reads, "In addition to all this, take up the shield of faith, with which you can extinguish all the flaming arrows of the evil one." That word *all* is huge, isn't it?

Your faith is the chemistry and dynamics of your relationship with God. It's you and God walking together. It's walking with God into eternity. Faith is not a feeling. It's not something you drum up, sing up, shout up, or praise up. Rather, it's something that develops based on relationship.

As you live with a person over a period of years, a certain relationship forms. You have faith in that person. I have faith in my wife, and she has faith in me. That means we trust each other. For example, I'm not wondering right now if Barb is being faithful to me. For another example, I often make decisions for the both of us, even when Barb's not present. I do so confidently, because I know her and I know the dynamics of our relationship. I keep faith with her.

As we walk with God, we become people of faith. Not because

we have accepted a particular theological doctrine. Not because we just got pumped up at a rally. Rather, it's because we have come to know him. God and I have lived together now for over fifty years. That's a long time. The faith I have is based on the relationship that has emerged from this experience.

Whatever Satan shoots at you from his arsenal (and he'll fire everything he can!) is extinguished not by fancy footwork, but by your relationship with God—a relationship that Satan simply can't penetrate. He can throw the ugliest and worst at you. He can offer the most attractive and tempting to you. But because you have a vital, ongoing relationship with God, Satan's plan ultimately can't work. You have been walking with God. You trust him. He keeps faith with you, and you keep faith with him.

When you're in the most difficult place you can be, the pressure is on, and the temptations are flying, your faith is what takes the energy out of the attack. The arrows hit your shield and bounce off. Your faith in God puts their fire out, neutralizing their ability to inflict harm on you and the people around you.

The Helmet of Salvation

Paul gives us our next piece of armor in verse 17: "Take the helmet of salvation." That word *salvation* means wholeness, completeness. Why do we need it as a helmet? Because we need wholeness in our minds! When you allow God to direct your thoughts and keep your reasoning straight and true, you're thinking as a whole person would. You're not thinking with the fracturedness of a world that's in rebellion and chaos—a world that can't finish its sentences, let alone finish its thoughts. Instead, you're bringing godly understanding, wisdom, and thoughtfulness to your life and to the lives around you. You're thinking with the mind of Christ.

When Satan confronts a believer who thinks with the mind of Christ, he's pushed himself right up against a brick wall; he can go no further. That's why you need to have your own theology (grounded, of course, in the Word of God). You need to think it through for yourself. You need to know what you believe, not what I believe. What I believe will not stand up for you when Satan attacks; only what you believe will stand up for you on that day.

What is your own personal theology? Is it based on the truth of the Bible? Why do you serve God? What is he like to you? If he stopped answering your prayers, would you still serve him? If he stopped meeting your needs, would you still serve him? Why? *Think.*

As a pastor I don't want to teach people *what* to think; I want to help people think for themselves. I want them to use their renewed minds and begin to think Christianly. All around us we see huge amounts of "nonthink" in Jesus's name—things that don't make sense at all. We see hateful people yelling at each other in Jesus's name from both sides of an issue. We see others trying to define Christianity in terms of a political party, as though it were more Christian to be Republican or Democrat. Who are these people? Where is Jesus? *Think.*

Some time ago a group of people in our area gathered to sing through underwater speakers to whales. Watching the news clips, I couldn't help but think, *We curse each other, we commit road rage on the highways, we shoot each other, but we sing to whales. This is a strange world!*

That's why you need to have the helmet of salvation firmly in place. This is a strange, confused world. You need to be able to look at things Christianly and think Christianly. When fads come along that have the right name but the wrong content, you can see them for what they are. When some people are yelling this and other people are yelling that, you can approach the matter with the mind of Christ. If you have your helmet on, Satan cannot penetrate your mind with his worldly, twisted thinking.

The Sword of the Spirit

Verse 17 continues: "and [take] the sword of the Spirit, which is the word of God." The power of the Word of God against Satan's strategies is graphically displayed in the desert encounter between Jesus and the devil (see Matthew 4:1–11). Each temptation Jesus faced was an effort on Satan's part to get Jesus to achieve legitimate results in illegitimate ways.

If only rocks could become bread and feed the famished and dying!

If only God would give a graphic and spectacular demonstration of his power!

If only earthly power could be achieved without effort or sacrifice!

At every point Jesus's reply began with, "It is written . . ." Jesus established for all time: Expedience will not rule. Immediate felt needs will not trump the firm boundaries of the Word of God. Satan cannot enter here. His strategies cannot work where the Word of God reigns.

The sword of the Spirit is more than quoting Scripture, however. It is hearing God's voice clearly above the myriad of other voices screaming and demanding equal time. It is living consistently, even stubbornly, within the boundaries his voice defines. It is maintaining an unwavering commitment to the absolutes of his intention. There is truth. There are boundaries. Right and wrong can be identified, and right can be chosen.

Ours is a world of individualism, ethical and social relativism, and the pursuit of unhampered personal rights. Truth is fluid; commitment is conditional; greed rules. This is the environment that welcomes and promotes Satan's schemes. Like bacteria in a laboratory, his strategies thrive and multiply, unhindered and unquestioned, in such a culture.

That, however, is not *your* environment. As a child of God, you have boundaries. You understand absolutes. You have means other than your emotions and felt needs to evaluate right and wrong. When you are strategically placed in the face of one of Satan's ploys, it is just like Jesus saying, "It is written."

> **The sword of the Spirit is more than quoting Scripture.**

I talked recently with a young and very successful career woman, who told me about a high-level corporate meeting she attended in another city. One evening a surprise outing was planned for the whole group. After dinner the show started. She was shocked and insulted by the content. Had she been given the option, she would have chosen not to attend. She was not only upset by the entertainment; she was also bitterly disappointed in the people she had worked with for many years. They all seemed not only to approve but to enjoy the whole affair.

As I listened to her describe the situation, I thought, *Why not just get up and walk out?* We have all been in situations where the right thing to do demanded a quick exit or a firm confrontation. Laura Bush stood up and walked out of a banquet one night when the evening's jokes became coarse and offensive. What a statement for the First Lady to make!

"I thought of just getting up and walking out," the woman said, as if she had read my mind. "The problem was that we were a long way from our hotel, we had all come together, and that street at night was no place for a woman to be alone."

She continued, "I suppose walking out could still have been an option. But I realized I was not so much concerned about myself as I was disturbed about the enthusiasm of my coworkers. Was there a way to not only register my displeasure but also make sure something like that never happened again in our workplace?"

She prayed and decided the best thing to do was to register her concern with her boss. Her objection was not a judgment on what the others did. Rather, she objected to being forced to participate in something that violated her values. Furthermore, she was concerned that such activity worked against the environment they were trying to establish in their company.

Because of the high regard she enjoys from her boss, both for her character and her work, she found an open door and an open mind. She discovered her boss had been equally uncomfortable, but he had been unwilling to do anything about it. He was very sympathetic to her view; in fact, he said he had expected her to diplomatically raise the issue with him. He assured her nothing similar would be a part of any future meetings.

Understand, this was not just one person registering a complaint. It wasn't a Christian whining about sinners sinning. This was a strategically placed covenant believer taking up the sword of the Spirit and establishing boundaries beyond which Satan can no longer go. This woman can't control what her coworkers do on their own time, nor does she want to. But as far as their workplace is concerned, they will no longer be exposed to such evil. Whatever next step Satan had in mind to pollute this group of people has been effectively thwarted.

Of course, there are times when different actions are needed. But being with sinners does not necessitate participating in their sin. I'm sure when Jesus was accused of being a "glutton and a drunkard" (Matthew 11:19), it was not because he was falling down drunk. It was because he was in the company of those who were. The sword of the Spirit helps you define God's intention and hear his word for your situation. When you hear and respond, Satan's schemes are frustrated.

Pray in the Spirit

Finally, Paul enjoins us to "pray in the Spirit on all occasions with all kinds of prayers and requests" (Ephesians 6:18). That seems reasonable, don't you think? If you are this remarkable covenant person, strategically placed by Christ to (1) continue his redeeming work on earth, (2) frustrate Satan's plans, and (3) block the tsunami of evil, you had better learn to pray! You had better learn to pray in the Spirit, and you had better know how to pray all kinds of prayers for all occasions.

The overall impotence of the church's prayer life today is not due to a lack of technique; it's due to a lack of engagement with the enemy.

A new recruit and a seasoned veteran were bouncing along the road in a transport truck headed for the front lines. They could hear the bombs and gunfire ahead. The young private confessed to the vet, "I wish I'd done better with my rifle on the firing range." To which the older soldier replied, "Your aim tends to improve when someone's firin' back."

When we lounge in the safety of our Christian ideals and beg for our comfort to be increased, our safety ensured, and our treasures increased, our prayers easily become pitiful, rambling, religious drivel. But when we begin to see ourselves as the church on Monday, strategically placed in the path of a treacherous flood of evil, the aim and impact of our prayers is dramatically improved. No mere cerebral, prayerlike exercise will do! Spirit must communicate with Spirit and respond prophetically, compassionately, and redemptively.

"Pray in the Spirit on all occasions with all kinds of prayers" describes the church engaged, not the church at rest. No more whining out loud in Jesus's name and labeling it prayer! We have destiny; we have purpose. God is about his glorious plan, and he has included us. It is prayer that causes us to see what he is doing and join him. It is prayer that exposes our vulnerability and directs us to safety. It is prayer that enables us to hear what God is saying and say it; to see what he sees and respond as Jesus would.

Now do you see why Jesus taught us to pray, "Lead us not into temptation, but deliver us from evil" (Matthew 6:13)? The temptation is at hand. The evil is up to your waist. And what about, "Your kingdom come, your will be done on earth as it is in heaven" (Matthew 6:10)? This is a critical prayer when you understand your strategic assignment as light in a dark and confused world. The same words are hollow in the echoing hallways of mere religious activity.

As we've said before, we live in evil days. That's why today, tomorrow, and every day, you need to remember: God has equipped you with spiritual armor specifically designed to frustrate Satan's plans and stop evil in its tracks. The Bible says, "When the enemy comes in like a flood, the Spirit of the LORD will lift up a standard against him" (Isaiah 59:19 NKJV). Are you ready to be that standard, in Jesus's name? If your answer is yes, then welcome to the church on Monday!

GOD'S PLAN
for
YOU

Dream with me for a moment. *What if everything we've talked about in the last fourteen chapters is true? What if you and I really begin to think and act like the church on Monday? What if God really does live in us and, by the power of the Holy Spirit, can live through us? What if we really are who he says we are: people of covenant and destiny and purpose? What if we really are strategically positioned in places where Jesus's life can be released and Satan's strategies can be neutralized?*

It's preposterous! Only God could think up a plan like that . . .

We've been talking about the principles of being the church in the world. We've said that while the church on Sunday is extremely important, what happens on Sunday is not the primary work of the church. The assembly of the church is meant to equip and encourage and enhance the *real* work of the church, which doesn't take place within the four walls of a sanctuary. It takes place on the highways and byways and in the workplaces and meeting places of the world.

THE MONDAY MORNING CHURCH

To me, Monday is the most important day of the week. That's when we invade again, infiltrate again; we go back to those places where Christ, the Lord of the church, has strategically placed us. Some of those places are enjoyable. Some of those places are disturbing, disgusting, and difficult.

All that matters is that you're where Jesus has asked you to be. God's will for you is not based on your comfort or pleasure. Rather, it's based on a single idea: did Jesus ask you to do this? If he did, then do it! Did he lead you to where you are? If he did, then stay there!

Remember, you have a place called heaven to rest up in. You can reserve the first one-third of eternity for R&R if you want; but down here on earth, you are not called to rest, comfort, and ease. There's a time for that, but this isn't it! So if you're in a job with a bunch of bad people who curse and swear and tell coarse jokes, I don't feel a bit sorry for you. They're probably the reason you're there.

Here's what I want so very much for you: When you go back into your world on Monday, I want you to go back with an awareness of who you are and who lives in you. I want you to live up to your true identity as a covenant child of God. When you catch yourself living below that identity, say, "Thank you, Jesus, for showing me where I'm falling short. Help me now to become the new person you've made me to be."

I want you to be OK with wherever he has put you. Your job right now may not be the one you'd choose, but it may well be the job he has chosen for you. I want you to have just one prayer as you start your day: "Lord, give me somebody to bless. Give me somebody to be kind to today. Give me somebody to help today.

Give me someone who is thirsty today, so I can give a cup of cold water in your name."

That's the kind of prayer that makes you "open for business." It's the kind of lifestyle that shows Jesus to the world—the Jesus that a large percentage of the world has never seen. The Jesus they will be attracted to. The Jesus who magnetizes people to himself.

This is the Jesus who lives in us through his Spirit. This is the Jesus who died for every person you will ever meet. This is the Jesus who seeks to love and redeem these fallen and broken people. He is coming to them through you.

So be yourself. Be filled with him. Be open for business.

You are the church on Monday.

NOTES

Introduction: The POWER of the CHURCH on MONDAY

1. E. Stanley Jones, *The Christ of the Indian Road* (Nashville: Abingdon Press, 1925), 28.

Chapter 3: Where CONFIDENCE BEGINS

1. John Powell, *Why Am I Afraid to Tell You Who I Am?* (Niles, Ill.: Argus Communications, 1969), 12.

Chapter 11: A WORTHY LIFE

1. The question is the title to the classic book by Francis Schaeffer: *How Should We Then Live? The Rise and Decline of Western Thought and Culture* (Wheaton, Ill.: Crossway Books, 1983).

Printed in the United States
By Bookmasters